W9-AFT-091

Praise for *The Mercy Prayer*

"Robert Gelinas reminds us that God's love is the orientation to life, the air we breathe, and the sky above us—not something we earn or deserve but something God graces upon us because God loves us."

— Scot McKnight, professor of New Testament, Northern Seminary, author of *The King Jesus Gospel*

"In *The Mercy Prayer* Pastor Robert Gelinas shows why he is recognized in Denver as one of the true spiritual fathers of our city. His explanation of the prayer that God always answers is life-giving and life-changing and has the power to change a community."

— Geoff Surratt, managing director, *Exponential*

"Robert Gelinas doesn't just teach or talk about mercy—he is the living embodiment of one of God's greatest gifts. This book will awaken your heart's cry for mercy and readiness to extend it to others."

— Margaret Feinberg, author of *Wonderstruck* (www. margaretfeinberg.com)

"In *The Mercy Prayer*, Robert Gelinas revolutionizes our prayer lives by challenging us to boldly ask for what God is waiting to grant: his mercy. This book has made *the* most prayed prayer in the Bible, *my* most prayed prayer in life."

— Elisa Morgan, publisher, *FullFill*; speaker; author of *The Beauty of Broken: My Story and Likely Yours Too* (www. elisamorgan.com)

"Robert Gelinas dives deep into the biblical waters of understanding God's mercy and revolutionary love for us. His practical theology and insightful examples provide a wonderful resource for Christian formation. May readers be led to the daily journey of the transformational gift this book explores."

— Efrem Smith, Regional Catalyst with the Evangelical Covenant Church; author of *The Post-Black and Post-White Church*

"Both challenging and captivating, this arresting reflection on the mercy we receive from God invites us, in turn, to grant mercy to the hurting and desperate travelers in our own lives. Timely and redeeming. Healing and beautiful. Conceived and written as only Robert Gelinas could do it. A book to keep and share."

— Patricia Raybon, author of *My First White Friend* and *I Told the Mountain to Move*

"We live in a world that is thirsty for mercy and hungry for grace. My friend, Pastor Robert, does a remarkable job of showing that God wants to give both in abundance. This book is healing, helpful, and hopeful."

— Pastor Brady Boyd, New Life Church, Colorado Springs; author of *Sons and Daughters*

"I've been singing *kyrie eleison* nearly every Sunday since I was a child in the Lutheran church, but hadn't really reflected on the significance of this prayer until I read Robert's book. I can't wait to sing it again next Sunday, with a whole new perspective. In our work among Denver's homeless, we are always on the lookout for resources to give hope to those who struggle on the margins of society, as well as those who serve in hard places. Robert writes with our people in mind. This book is full of hope."

— Dr. Jeff Johnsen, executive director of Mile High Ministries, Denver; ordained member of the Street Psalms Community

"Fifty years from now, if Christians are widely known as merciful people who have a passion for God and a commitment to justice, people who easily and freely esteem their neighbors above themselves, then Robert Gelinas and his family will be remembered as pioneers who helped show us the way."

— Dr. Miriam Dixon, pastor, Golden First Presbyterian Church

"Robert Gelinas lives his life under the strong and enduring promise of God's mercy. This makes his prayer more than a lifeline . . . but rather of way of life. *The Mercy Prayer* ushers the faithful follower and the skeptic to a place where they have a front row seat to the character of God and the message of Jesus. Ringing from the pages of scripture and echoing the heart of God—yes, Lord, have mercy."

— Dan Wolgemuth, president and
CEO, Youth for Christ USA

"*The Mercy Prayer* appears to be a small, easily read volume. Do not be deceived! I found myself stopping to reflect, to pray, to think about where I am in the book and where others I know and love are. Within one day I could easily have given out five copies. *The Mercy Prayer* is a book whose time has come for this generation. Many thanks to Robert Gelinas for sharing his wisdom and deep faith with us, his readers."

— Deborah Rillos, Director of
Spiritual Formation, Golden
First Presbyterian Church

"I have known Robert for over 20 years and he has always had an uncanny ability to make the Scriptures come alive. What do you do when you are suffering? When temptation has besieged you? When you are in pain? You ask for mercy. In the pleading, 'We are asking God to step in, to look at our situation, and supernaturally intrude upon our circumstances and change the course of our lives' (p. 90). Knowing Robert the way I do, these are not only his words, this is how he has lived his life. He embodies the mercy. I highly recommend this book because it represents a life of study in God's deepest mercies, and a life of living God's deepest mercies."

— The Rev. Stace Timothy
Tafoya, rector, Church of the
Epiphany, Denver

"If ever a generation needed the renewed awareness of a God who is forever 'rich in mercy,' it is now! Robert Gelinas masterfully compels us to pray out, breathe in, and pass on the comfort and assurance that God hears our cries for mercy and faithfully comes to our relief. A powerful reminder to restore hope. God's intervention is just a plea away."

— Dwight Robertson, president,
Kingdom Building Ministries;
author of *You Are God's Plan A*

"I've whispered my own desperate pleas for mercy. I've sat with others as they cried for relief. But not until reading *The Mercy Prayer* have I seen how elemental this form of communion with God really is—pulsing with every beat of our hearts."

— Scott Dewey, codirector, Center
for Transforming Mission

"In *The Mercy Prayer*, Robert Gelinas reminds us that prayer is not only a practice but a relationship. Both pastoral and profound in spirit, Gelinas reveals how God uses this relationship to transform our perspectives so that we can better share his mercy with others. This excellent book will revolutionize your ministry by revolutionizing your life."

— Edward Gilbreath, author
of *Reconciliation Blues* and
Birmingham Revolution

The
Mercy
PRAYER

The One Prayer Jesus *Always* Answers

ROBERT GELINAS

THOMAS NELSON
Since 1798

NASHVILLE DALLAS MEXICO CITY RIO DE JANEIRO

© 2013 by Robert Gelinas

All rights reserved. No portion of this book may be reproduced, stored in a retrieval system, or transmitted in any form or by any means—electronic, mechanical, photocopy, recording, scanning, or other—except for brief quotations in critical reviews or articles, without the prior written permission of the publisher.

Published in Nashville, Tennessee, by Thomas Nelson. Thomas Nelson is a registered trademark of Thomas Nelson, Inc.

Published in association with the literary agency of Wolgemuth & Associates, Inc.

Thomas Nelson, Inc., titles may be purchased in bulk for educational, business, fund-raising, or sales promotional use. For information, please e-mail SpecialMarkets@ThomasNelson.com.

Unless otherwise indicated, Scripture quotations are taken from the Holy Bible, New International Version®, NIV®. Copyright © 1973, 1978, 1984, 2011 by Biblica, Inc.™ Used by permission of Zondervan. All rights reserved worldwide. www.zondervan.com.

Scripture quotations marked NKJV are from THE NEW KING JAMES VERSION. © 1982 by Thomas Nelson, Inc. Used by permission. All rights reserved.

Scripture quotations marked KJV are from the King James Version of the Bible.

Library of Congress Cataloging-in-Publication Data

Gelinas, Robert, 1969–
  The mercy prayer : the one prayer Jesus always answers / Robert Gelinas.
    pages cm
  Includes bibliographical references.
  ISBN 978-1-4002-0445-8
  1. Jesus prayer. 2. God (Christianity)—Mercy. I. Title.
  BT590.J28G45 2013
  231'.6—dc22   2012049563

Printed in the United States of America

13 14 15 16 17 RRD 6 5 4 3 2 1

For those who sin and those

who suffer. For those who suffer

because of sin. For those who

sin to alleviate their suffering.

Lord, have mercy on us.

Contents

Foreword

I n recent years a number of best-selling books have been written to discredit belief in God. Authored by advocates of so-called "New Atheism," they have assumed our culture's pervasive religious question is, "Does God exist?" The fact that nearly 9 in 10 people continue to believe in God shows they've misunderstood the core dilemma of the human condition. Most of us are not asking, "Does God exist?" but rather, "Is God good?" We want to know if we can trust God enough to surrender our lives and our loves to his care. With a pastor's heart and an intuitive wisdom, Robert Gelinas sees our need and has produced a book that isn't merely about prayer, but the character of the God who hears them.

He recognizes that the cry for mercy is as old as

humanity and it expresses a longing at the core of our condition. It is a cry that emerges from our shared experience of an unpredictable and seemingly indifferent world. Amid the inevitable pain of life we pray for mercy because our spirits refuse to succumb to the darkness. We writhe at the thought that our pain is devoid of meaning or witness. So we call out to God not merely for evidence of his presence, but for proof that there remains a light behind the shadow we are experiencing. "Lord, have mercy!" is more than a cry for help. It is a cry for love. Through it we are not simply asking, "God, will you help me?" We are asking, "God, do you love me?" Through the testimony of Scripture, Gelinas shows us that the resounding answer to that question is "Yes!"

Of course the darkness we strive against is not confined to the world we inhabit. When a newspaper invited noted authors to submit essays on the question "What is wrong with the world today?" G. K. Chesterton provided the shortest response:

> Dear Sirs,
> I am.
> Yours, G. K. Chesterton

We are not just victims in the unfolding cosmic drama; we are very often the villains. We need to be rescued from ourselves as much as from our circumstances. Does the goodness of God extend to those of us who have *caused* and not simply experienced the pain of this world?

This may be where Gelinas offers us the most hopeful vision of God. He brings definition and clarity to the portrait of God that has become hazy in our day. Gelinas shows us a merciful, forgiving judge whose love does not ignore justice, and whose justice is animated by love. He transports us to scenes where Jesus touches sinners, speaks with failures, and redeems traitors. In each one we can see ourselves receiving the mercy we know we need from a God who never hesitates to provide it.

I hope you read this book slowly and reflectively, allowing the fears and pains you've suppressed to emerge. Be honest about the nagging doubts you've carried about God's love and goodness. And express them to him with the simple words that have passed the lips of countless saints before you: "Lord, have mercy." On the other side of this prayer you will find more than an answer. You will find Christ himself.

Skye Jethani
May 2013

ONE

The Most Prayed Prayer

No judge wants to be labeled "soft on crime."

Judges are supposed to be fair, unbiased, and impartial, but in the end, tough. They are to make sure criminals and wrongdoers pay their debts to society. Judges aren't praised for giving minimal jail time to a drug dealer or probation to a habitual offender. In a land with three-strikes laws and voters who don't take kindly to plea bargains, being known as a judge who lets offenders off with a slap on the wrist is not a good thing. Judges are expected to lay down the law to lawbreakers; to be tough on crime. And when they aren't, they gain a bad reputation.

For example, many people were angry with Judge Reichbach in New York City for being too easy on criminals. When Dominick Bunch stood before him in court because he'd been caught selling an illegal firearm, prosecutors asked for a five-year prison sentence. Even though the defendant admitted to the crime, the judge reduced his sentence to a mere six months in jail plus six months of probation.

"It's an absolute outrage; he should be ashamed of himself," said the district attorney.

"This young man is deserving of a break," said the judge.[1]

If you relent in your punishment of criminals, prosecutors will try to avoid your courtroom and request that you remove yourself from their cases. When it's election time, your adversaries will run ads against you stirring up the ire of voters. Someone might even start a petition to force your resignation.

A lenient judge invites outrage and indignation. That's what bothered my grandmother about God.

A Good God with a Bad Reputation

Before I was in kindergarten, Grandma made sure that I was in Sunday school. I am grateful for those formative years of learning the Scriptures and understanding the gospel because they ultimately resulted in my coming to faith.

Every Sunday I'd put on my suit with the dark-green pants and the light-green coat. It was adorned with all the pins that I earned from memorizing Bible verses and keeping perfect attendance. Then my grandmother would drive me to the church, park the car out front, and send me in to learn about God. She, on the other hand, would stay in the car.

At the end of class, even if it was cold and snowing, I would walk out to find the car parked in the same spot. I'd hop in, and we'd head for home.

In my teen years I asked her why she never went to church. This was the beginning of many conversations that always ended with her exclaiming, "You mean to tell me that a mafia hit man has just as good a chance to go to heaven as I do?" She couldn't get past the idea that someone worse than her could end up with her in paradise. It was an affront to her sense of justice.

Grandma was on to something: God is soft on crime. Murderers, adulterers, and habitual offenders have entered his court and walked away scot-free. Now if you are a prosecutor, this might seem like bad news. But if you are the criminal—a wrongdoer, a reprobate, a sinner—then it's a different story.

For us habitual offenders, God's infamously bad reputation is truly good news.

The Theme Is Mercy

Mercy is a—perhaps *the*—theme of my life. On November 6, 1969, I was born at Denver's Mercy Hospital. It's been torn down and replaced by high-end condos, but anyone who's from Denver knows where the old Mercy was located. My wife and I have six children. One of our daughters, who is from Ethiopia, is named Mihret. In Amharic her name means "Mercy of God."

Mercy is also perhaps *the* theme of Scripture. God's mercy is on display again and again in virtually every book of the Bible.

After leading the Israelites from Egypt, Moses turned to God in need of assurance. He doubted himself and his ability to lead Israel to the promised land. He cried out, wanting to know if God was pleased with him and if God would continue to lead him and the Israelites.

God responded to his servant in a most unique way: he put his name on display. In the Hebrew mind, to know someone's name was to know their character. "I will cause all my goodness to pass in front of you," said God, "and I will proclaim my name, the LORD, in your presence" (Ex. 33:19). God is the Lord. He has many names, but when we see "LORD" in all caps, a very specific name of God is being used: "I Am." That is the name God originally gave to Moses at the burning bush. It means, simply, God is. It's a statement of his eternal nature—that God always was and always will be. But it is more than that; it also means all that God is, always was, and always will be. That is, all God's attributes are also eternal, including his mercy.

Moses needed to know that the God who is, was with him. So God said he would pass in front of him and proclaim his name. Another way to think of this is that God was going to give a sermon about his name— the word *proclaim* is synonymous with *preach*. What text did God choose for his sermon? His mercy: "I will have mercy on whom I will have mercy, and I will have compassion on whom I will have compassion" (Ex. 33:19). To know God's name is to know God's mercy and that his mercy always was, is, and will be.

God's mercy is one of the central themes of Scripture, especially in the Old Testament. I often hear people make the false dichotomy that in the Old Testament God is a God of wrath and in the New Testament he is a God of love. This simply isn't true. Mercy is not something that shows up only in the New Testament. For example, note that all these verses are found in the Old Testament:

- For the LORD your God is a merciful God; he will not abandon or destroy you. (Deut. 4:31)
- The LORD will turn from his fierce anger; he will show you mercy. (Deut. 13:17)
- But in your great mercy you did not put an end to them or abandon them, for you are a gracious and merciful God. (Neh. 9:31)
- Remember, O LORD, your great mercy and love, for they are from of old. (Ps. 25:6)
- Who is a God like you, who pardons sin and forgives the transgression of the remnant of his inheritance? You do not stay angry forever but delight to show mercy. (Mic. 7:18)

James Montgomery Boice remarked, "Have you found the mercy of God in the Word of God? Until you have, you will never think of the Bible as being wonderful."[2] Boice wrote those words in reference to the longest chapter in the Bible—Psalm 119.[3]

Pardon, Please

In his writings about the Psalms, James Montgomery Boice told the story of George Wishart. He was the bishop of Edinburgh in the sixteenth century and found himself sentenced to death in those unhappy times. It was customary to allow the condemned to choose a psalm to be sung before his or her execution. As the story goes, Wishart, knowing that a pardon was on its way, chose Psalm 119 because of its extraordinary length—176 verses in all. It was a good bet; before the psalm was finished the pardon arrived, and Wishart was spared from the gallows.

Psalm 119 is the most intricate of all the psalms because it is an acrostic poem. Composed of twenty-two stanzas, one for each letter of the Hebrew alphabet, virtually every verse refers to the virtues of God's Word: his laws and commandments. But one of the few verses that vary the subject, verse 132, is a request for the mercy of God: "Turn to me and have mercy on me, as you always do to those who love your name." Like Wishart, the psalmist is hoping for a pardon.

Mercy is the opposite of justice. Justice is what we deserve in any given situation. Mercy, on the other hand, is *not* receiving what we deserve, or receiving less than we have coming to us. God is just, but that is not what the psalmist is asking for in his situation. He desires mercy.

Notice his rationale: "as you always do to those who love your name." Essentially he says, "I see you pouring your mercy into the lives of everybody else around me. I would like some too." His request indicates that God has a reputation in the neighborhood. When you find yourself in God's courtroom, even though you stand before him guilty as charged, if you ask for mercy, then mercy you shall receive. So the psalmist says, "Give me some too." To quote the old hymn,

> Pass me not, O gentle Savior,
> Hear my humble cry;
> While on others thou art calling,
> Do not pass me by.[4]

Fortunately for the psalmist, God is indeed most merciful. He is known for being lavish with his clemency and compassion. In Scripture we see the mercy of God paraded in all its pageantry. David declares in Psalm 23, "Surely goodness and mercy shall follow me all the days of my life" (v. 6 KJV).

God himself promises in Isaiah:

> For the mountains shall depart
> And the hills be removed,
> But My kindness [mercy] shall not depart
>   from you,
> Nor shall My covenant of peace be removed,
> Says the LORD, who has mercy on you.
>
> (ISA. 54:10 NKJV)

I have lived in Colorado all my life. Mountains have been ever-present for me. They are how I navigate. Growing up in Denver, you gain an intuitive sense of where the mountains are. Even when the skies are overcast and I can't see them, I instinctively sense their presence and know which way is west. In this passage from Isaiah, God invites us to imagine a day—impossible though it might seem—when the Front Range of the Rockies disappears. Pikes Peak and all the other majestic "four-teeners" are gone. Ingrained as they are in my mind, it's almost inconceivable to imagine them away. They seem so stable and fixed.

Yet God says that the mountains are *fleeting* compared to his mercy; and while snow-covered peaks will pass away, God will never remove his mercy from our lives. As a matter of fact, God has an abundance of mercy (he's rich in it!), and he shares it with us generously (Eph. 2:4–5).

There is a chilling scene in the movie *Gladiator* where the emperor Commodus has discovered a plot to overthrow his government. His sister, Lucilla, was a part of the ruse, along with the hero of the story, Maximus. The emperor has Maximus jailed and then confronts his sister. He makes it known that she is not receiving the penalty she deserves, though he warns that if she even looks at him in a manner that displeases him, her son will die. Furthermore, he demands her love and intimacy in return.

He then asks twice, once in a whisper and then again with an angry yell, *"Am I not merciful?"*

That is not God. God does not dispense mercy with reluctance. When he grants this gift, he doesn't do so with a vengeful scowl that makes us feel as though we owe him. The Scriptures say that God "delight[s] to show mercy" (Mic. 7:18). He smiles when he sees an opportunity to bestow leniency upon someone, and he gains pleasure in offering pardon to those who come to him in need.

Mercy by Design

I admit it. Morbid curiosity caused me to pick up the book *How We Die: Reflections on Life's Final Chapter* by Dr. Sherwin Nuland. The title alone got me; I was curious about what would be in the pages of a book like this. After all, in our culture we have isolated death to hospitals and hospices, far from our normal lives. In his book, Dr. Nuland, a surgeon, gives a behind-the-scenes look at the end of life. It was more than a gratuitous, voyeuristic peek at death. I found it profound and thought provoking.

What happens when we die of a stroke? What is

the process we go through when we pass away due to a heart attack? What happens when we die of AIDS or cancer? The chapter on traumatic death stood out in particular. What happens when death sneaks up on us? What happens when it's not a slow-working disease but rather a violent act, something sudden and unexpected, that takes a life?

Dr. Nuland recounts the horrifyingly sad story of a young girl name Katie who was murdered. No need to go into the details except to say that her mom was nearby and saw what happened, but there was no way she could do anything. By the time little Katie's mom reached her side, the daughter was already passing from this life to the next. The mom just held her nine-year-old child and began to speak to her as she did when Katie was an infant.

Katie died as her mom looked into her face. Later her mom wrote about her daughter's expression at that moment. It wasn't what one would expect. Her muscles were obviously forming an expression, but it wasn't one of somebody who'd just gone through a trauma. There wasn't a look of terror. No sign of shock. Rather, her mom says, Katie's countenance actually matched a portrait they had taken in their home. It was peaceful and calm. What caused that—the disconnect between the facial expression and the kind of death occurring?

Dr. Nuland says that's actually something many people have noticed; when somebody is dying a traumatic death, there seems to be a moment when the body experiences something different from the trauma that is taking place. Those who have been involved in wars have reported what's known as battlefield euphoria. You have wounds, bullets in your body. You're bleeding and seriously injured, yet you are still fighting to live. You don't feel the pain and are still lucid.

Some say it's an ancient response humans have, and that it can be traced back to when we coexisted with prehistoric predators. We had to be on our guard, and adrenaline (to help us run fast) and endorphins (natural painkillers) were developed to help us live in this fight-or-flight world of fear. Maybe that's the explanation.

My preference is what David Livingstone concluded from his own firsthand experience with trauma. Livingstone was a missionary to South Africa in the 1800s. One day, when out walking through the jungle, his party came across a wounded lion. Hurt but not incapacitated, the lion attacked Livingstone, latching on to his left shoulder. It picked him up off the ground and began to shake him as a dog shakes a toy, as a cat shakes a rat. Thankfully one of his traveling companions frightened the animal away by firing both barrels of a rifle. Livingstone survived.

Upon reflection, Livingston said that what he perceived didn't match the situation. During the attack, he was calm. It was almost like slow motion. He said there was even a moment when he turned and looked the lion in the eye and felt no fear as he bled profusely. Even though he had major lacerations in his body, through muscle and to the bone, he felt no pain. It was completely out of context.

It's almost as if something stepped in and changed the course of events. What he was supposed to be experiencing, he wasn't. What do you call that? I like what David Livingstone called it. He names it *mercy*. He said, "This . . . is a merciful provision by our benevolent Creator for lessening the pain of death."[5]

Believe it! Our God is so merciful that he even built mercy into our biology. Even when we don't have time to ask, in a moment of trauma, he comes to our aid.

Multifaceted Mercy

In the Old Testament, the most used word for God's mercy is the Hebrew word *hesed*. However, God's *hesed* is so multifaceted that it takes more than one English word to describe it. That's why, in addition to being translated "mercy," it's also translated as a variety of other English words, depending on the context. You may also see it as "compassionate," "gracious," "slow to anger," "steadfast love," "unfailing love," "goodness," "generous love," and "loving-kindness." When the Scriptures speak of God as merciful, they're describing God taking action in our lives in what I've observed to be four different ways.

Mercy Is Compassion

Compassion is the kind of feeling a mother has for the child developing in her womb. Compassion is what causes her to smile when she feels her baby moving and kicking inside. It's a feminine kind of love. God feels for us in this way. As our Creator he knows what it means to conceive, nurture, and give birth. His mercy, when displayed in our lives, can be a gentle, womblike love of protection around our lives.

Mercy Is Grace

To say that God is gracious means that he has stooped down low and offered kindness to someone beneath him. Because God is the highest being in the universe, every form of interaction is for him a gracious act. When he receives the worship of the angels or listens to our prayers, he lowers himself; there is nothing equal to or higher than him. If in his mercy God did not come down to us, we could never know him. All knowledge we have about our Creator is a result of his gracious stooping to our level in word and in flesh.

Mercy Is Not Anger

Aren't you happy that God is slow to anger? Otherwise we would start looking for the lightning bolt as soon as we did something wrong. While we don't seek to displease God, neither do we fear that he's waiting to zap us when we fail. Scripture tells us that God is love.[6] It also tells us that love is patient.[7] We don't have to worry about immediate annihilation, because God is slow to anger.

Mercy Is God's Love

To say that God is merciful means that God "loves us as we are and not as we should be."[8] In this life we will never be "as we should be." The day will come when we are perfected in God's presence, but God won't wait until then to love us—you might even say he *can't*. He must love us now! To wait to love us would mean waiting too long for God; instead, he chooses to love us as we are. It's the expression of his nature.

These are the four different ways God's mercy is displayed in our lives. Many times they appear together in Scripture. In the story we looked at earlier, for instance, when God passed before Moses he referred to himself as "the compassionate and gracious God, slow to anger, abounding in love and faithfulness, maintaining love to thousands, and forgiving wickedness, rebellion and sin" (Ex. 34:6–7). All four facets of God's mercy are found in Psalm 103 as well: "The LORD is compassionate and gracious, slow to anger, abounding in love" (v. 8). But let's get practical. If God is all these things, then what can we expect from him? The psalmist continues:

> He will not always accuse,
>> nor will he harbor his anger forever;
> he does not treat us as our sins deserve
>> or repay us according to our iniquities.
> For as high as the heavens are above the earth,
>> so great is his love for those who fear him;
> as far as the east is from the west,
>> so far has he removed our transgressions
>> from us.
>
> (Ps. 103:9–12)

God's mercy is magnificent and multifaceted. Because it is a dominant theme in my life, I've thought a lot about it. The source of my passion for God's mercy is not just a result of the odd coincidence of my birthplace and my explaining to Mihret the meaning of her name. No, it runs far deeper.

You see, it seems to me that either God is merciful or God simply doesn't exist.

What If the Opposite Were True?

Can you imagine if God were not merciful? Try to fathom a life in which the natural consequences of everything we did wrong turned up like bills in the mail. Who could survive knowing that the tidal wave of our regrets was bearing down upon us? As the psalmist asks, "If you, O LORD, kept a record of sins, O Lord, who could stand?" (Ps. 130:3). Mercy means that God is not treating us as our sins deserve. God is not keeping a tally. He is not accusing. Not harboring. Not repaying us for our wrongs. If he did, none of us could survive. None of us is perfect.

That's what made Jonah so angry. One day God told him that he wanted him to go deliver a message to the Ninevites. Jonah didn't want to go. Who could blame him? The Ninevites were evil people. They practiced perverted sex acts in their worship of idols. Ninevah was known to be a bloody city with a reputation for the horrible things its inhabitants did to other human beings. So one could understand if Jonah had walked out his front door and headed the opposite direction of Nineveh; he was afraid of what its residents might do to him. But that wasn't it. Jonah ran, but he was not running scared.

Traveling the opposite direction of Nineveh, he went to sea, where he was thrown overboard in a storm and swallowed alive by a giant fish. Now facing certain death, Jonah finally gave in. He would go to Nineveh. The fish vomited Jonah onto dry ground, and he traveled inland with God's message for Nineveh: "The Almighty is unhappy with the life you are living."[9] The people repented and God relented.

So Jonah was pleased, right? Unfortunately, no. Jonah exploded at God, saying essentially, "The reason I didn't want to come here is because I knew your reputation!" He cited the four facets of God's mercy as proof: "I knew that you are a gracious and compassionate God, slow to anger and abounding in love, a God who relents from sending calamity" (Jonah 4:2). Jonah would have preferred the Ninevites get what he figured they had coming. He figured he was better than they were. But true to form, God was merciful and spared the city.

How do we explain all the wrong that goes unpunished? Was my grandmother correct in her dismay that a mafia hit man could end up with God, unpunished for his terrible deeds? What about the Ninevites? When we see a wrongdoer, do we mutter under our breath, "In the end, they'll get what's coming to them"? But can we be so sure?

I believe God exists. I live to lead people to Christ and a deeper understanding of the God who created them and loves them more deeply than they could ever hope. But if I were to come up with an argument against God's existence it would be this: There is an incredible lack of justice in this world. All too often evil—at all levels—goes unpunished.

I'm not talking about the problem of evil—that is, "If God is good, then why do bad things happen?" No, the cross has taught me that God can redeem even the greatest suffering. Rather, my struggle is with the problem of injustice and its accompanying question: "If God is just, then why does evil go unchecked?"

Gary Haugen has seen firsthand the wrong we humans perpetrate on each other. He writes:

> Such injustice is the plague of our earth. . . . Immoral soldiers take people's dignity, freedom, health and well-being through beatings, torture and incarceration. Corrupt authorities and moneylenders rob children of their childhood, health, innocence and joy through abusive servitude. Wealthy landowners rob widows of their land, livelihood and dignity. Brutal bigots in positions of power take away the loved ones, the livelihood and even the very lives of those who are of a different race, religion, gender or culture.[10]

Martin Luther King Jr. was right when he penned these words from the Birmingham City Jail: "Injustice anywhere is a threat to justice everywhere."[11] That's why we care for the poor, provide families and homes for orphans, and fight for the wrongfully accused who sit on death row. The incredible inequities we see in this world give us reasons to pool our money together and send teams of engineers to far-off lands to provide safe drinking water to those who don't have it. When we hear the stories our missionaries tell of the suffering they have seen, we know that all too many times it could have been avoided if only those in power used their power for good instead of evil.

Will they get what's coming to them?

Sometimes I stand with my jaw open like the older brother who arrives home after working yet another day in the hot sun and walks in on a barbecue dinner cooked in honor of his wayward brother (Luke 15:11–32). It's not fair. Yet I know in my heart that Jesus hopes all who have turned their noses up at the Father will return home and be welcomed back into the house with full rights and privileges.

Again, I'm not so caught up in why there is suffering in this world. We live in a fallen state. The Scriptures say, "God is love" and "God is just" (1 John 4:8; 2 Thess. 1:6). But, oh, how grateful I am that God is merciful as well. For either God doesn't exist, which would explain why so much evil goes unpunished, or God does exist, and what we are seeing is his mercy poured out daily upon his creation in immeasurable quantities.

So many people do bad things and are not punished—me included! So if I make this more personal, either God doesn't exist or God is merciful—otherwise, how do I explain all the wrong I have done that has gone seemingly unnoticed?

The Most Answered Prayer

I know a great deal about the mercy of God because I have firsthand experience with the Judge himself. I have stood in the line that leads into his courtroom more than I want to admit. I have found my seat in the crowded gallery and observed for myself how he deals with those who have done wrong. I have verified for myself that our good God deserves his bad reputation!

In the courtroom of the Scriptures, I have seen his mercy in action as murderers, adulterers, slanderers, and outcasts stand before him all with one simple request: *Lord, have mercy*—the most prayed prayer in the Bible.

- "Lord, have mercy" was the shout of blind men sitting roadside with nothing to lose. (Matt. 9:27; 20:30)

- "Lord, have mercy" was what ten numb lepers cried from a distance, energized with the hope of a new life. (Luke 17:13 NKJV)
- "Lord, have mercy" was the petition of a foreign Canaanite woman when she wanted Jesus to heal her suffering daughter. (Matt. 15:22)
- "Lord, have mercy" was the plea of King David in times of fear, in moments when he bordered on insanity, and at points when he put his kingdom at risk. This "man after [God's] own heart" (Acts 13:22) asked for mercy more than anyone else in the Bible.

Lord, have mercy is the most prayed prayer in the Bible. And get this: there is not one time in the Bible where God denies this request!

This is the most prayed prayer because God—the just and all-powerful Creator—is most merciful. He delights to show leniency to people. Throughout the Scriptures, God lavishly dispenses his loving-kindness. Many have experienced the life-altering effects of the mercy prayer.

Terry is a homeless man whose knees are so damaged that his biggest challenge each day is crossing the street before the light turns traffic against him. He and I have had many conversations. When he's drunk, he screams at God at the top of his lungs. One time he was screaming at me, "I'm just a gnat to God! In the same way I crush a bug, God has crushed me!" When the alcohol wore off, I asked Terry if he wanted to know what the most answered prayer in the Bible was. He did, and he has been one of my proofreaders for this book.

I have seen the mercy of God—and the process of seeking it—transform many, from sixteen-year-old sex addicts to men who are living with the consequences of ruining their marriages. One time, I saw a man sitting on a curb weeping uncontrollably. He couldn't speak. All I knew to do was to sit next to him, wrap my arms around his shoulders, and whisper, "God is merciful and desires to lessen your pain. Pray with me: Lord, have mercy . . . Lord, have mercy . . . Lord, have mercy." Sometimes just the act of praying the prayer is transformative. Just the recognition of the compassion, grace, and loving-kindness of God is enough to sooth a wounded soul. Just the anticipation of God's mercy is transformational in and of itself.

So let us immerse ourselves in the truth that God is compassionate, gracious, slow to anger, and abounding in love. Let us make the most prayed prayer of the Bible our most uttered request as well. Let us practice seeking God's mercy with every beat of our hearts, remembering that nowhere in the Bible does God deny a single request for mercy.

TWO

Echoes from Eternity

"Kyrie eleison."

It was the one sentence uttered to Jesus more than any other.

"*Kyrie eleison.*"

Those who traveled with Jesus heard it over and over.

"*Kyrie eleison.*"

We would have been amazed at the number and variety of people that came to Jesus and said, "*Kyrie eleison.*"

Some shouted it to Jesus from afar while others cried out up close. Some whispered the request while kneeling in humble respect, hoping Jesus would come to them.

Others frantically gave chase. Men and women; fathers and mothers; the outcast, desperate, and disabled—all called out to Jesus, for themselves and for their loved ones, "*Kyrie eleison*—Lord, have mercy."

The result? Jesus responded every single time. Not once did Jesus turn away this request. Rather, he stopped, delayed, inquired, healed, singled out of the crowd, and even expressed astonishment over the faith of those who asked. Christ reacted with compassion to every utterance of the mercy prayer.

Dispensing mercy was an essential part of his mission. To Jesus, showing compassion, granting grace, and alleviating suffering were not interruptions; they were central to his purpose. The disciples, however, felt differently. They seemed to think this request and Jesus' willingness to respond were getting in the way of the real business. But Jesus didn't seem wearied by it at all. On the contrary, he encouraged it.

Jesus told a parable about two people who went to the temple; one was a Pharisee and the other a tax collector. The Pharisee "stood up and prayed about himself." He pointed out to God all the wonderful things he had done for him, saying, "I fast twice a week and give a tenth of all I get." The other man stood at an unworthy distance and wouldn't even look up. In his shame before God, he pounded on his chest and simply said his own version of the most prayed prayer: "God, have mercy on me, a sinner" (Luke 18:9–13).

Jesus summarized the scenario by saying, "I tell you that this man, rather than the other, went home justified before God. For everyone who exalts himself will be humbled, and he who humbles himself will be exalted" (v. 14).

After this story, parents brought their children to Jesus to have him bless them, and blind men did everything they could to get his attention. By no means was Jesus annoyed by the mercy prayer. On the contrary, he fanned the flames.

Eternal Echoes

Fanny Crosby wrote more than eight thousand hymns. Though she lost her sight as an infant, she was deeply rooted in God's Word because she memorized large sections of Scripture. Instead of blaming the doctor whose mistake resulted in her darkness, she received it as a blessing. Fanny reasoned that when she arrived in heaven, the first face she would ever see would be that of her Savior. She once remarked that she might not have written all those songs if she had been distracted by the sights around her.

One day a friend played her a melody and asked

what the tune said. She responded, "Blessed assurance, Jesus is mine," and they proceeded to write one of her most loved hymns. Verse three is my favorite; in it she recognizes that God's willingness to dispense mercy reverberates throughout the pages of Scripture.[1] Fanny said it so well when she wrote,

> Perfect submission, perfect delight,
> Visions of rapture now burst on my sight;
> Angels descending, bring from above
> Echoes of mercy, whispers of love.[2]

I love the phrasing that only a sight-deprived yet audio-developed woman could come up with: "echoes of mercy."

Fanny Lou was in good company, for the people of God have a history of singing songs that proclaim his mercy. In 2 Chronicles 20 a powerful army was poised to attack God's people. Knowing that they had no hope of victory, Jehoshaphat called together all the men, women, and children, and in their presence he cried out to God. The Spirit of God told them to go out to their enemy and to "not be afraid or discouraged because of this vast army. For the battle is not yours, but God's" (v. 15). The next morning they bowed in worship before God, and as they headed out to the battlefield, Jehoshaphat asked some men to sing a simple chorus: "Praise the LORD, for His mercy endures forever" (v. 21 NKJV).

The Lord miraculously delivered them that day. The chorus that echoed on the battlefield was a regular part of worship for the people of God.[3] For example, in Psalm 100 they sang,

> Enter his gates with thanksgiving
>> and his courts with praise;
>> give thanks to him and praise his name.
> For the LORD is good and his love [mercy]
>> endures forever.
>
> (vv. 4–5)

This refrain is repeated in Psalm 106:

> Praise the LORD.
> Give thanks to the LORD, for he is good;
>> his love [mercy] endures forever.
>
> (v. 1)

Four more times in Psalm 118:

> Give thanks to the LORD, for he is good;
>> his love [mercy] endures forever

Let Israel say:
"His love [mercy] endures forever."
Let the house of Aaron say:
"His love [mercy] endures forever."
Let those who fear the Lord say:
"His love [mercy] endures forever."

(vv. 1–4)

By the time we get to Psalm 136 the refrain proclaiming the eternal nature of God's mercy is repeated twenty-six times in one song!

Oh, give thanks to the Lord, for He is good!
For His mercy endures forever.
Oh, give thanks to the God of gods!
For His mercy endures forever.
Oh, give thanks to the Lord of lords!
For His mercy endures forever:
To Him who alone does great wonders,
For His mercy endures forever;
To Him who by wisdom made the heavens,
For His mercy endures forever;
To Him who laid out the earth above the
waters,
For His mercy endures forever;

To Him who made great lights,
For His mercy endures forever—
The sun to rule by day,
For His mercy endures forever;
The moon and stars to rule by night,
For His mercy endures forever.
To Him who struck Egypt in their firstborn,
For His mercy endures forever;
And brought out Israel from among them,
For His mercy endures forever;
With a strong hand, and with an
outstretched arm,
For His mercy endures forever;
To Him who divided the Red Sea in two,
For His mercy endures forever;
And made Israel pass through the midst of it,
For His mercy endures forever;
But overthrew Pharaoh and his army in the
Red Sea,
For His mercy endures forever;
To Him who led His people through the
wilderness,
For His mercy endures forever;
To Him who struck down great kings,
For His mercy endures forever;

And slew famous kings,
　　For His mercy endures forever—
Sihon king of the Amorites,
　　For His mercy endures forever;
And Og king of Bashan,
　　For His mercy endures forever—
And gave their land as a heritage,
　　For His mercy endures forever;
A heritage to Israel His servant,
　　For His mercy endures forever.
Who remembered us in our lowly state,
　　For His mercy endures forever;
And rescued us from our enemies,
　　For His mercy endures forever;
Who gives food to all flesh,
　　For His mercy endures forever.
Oh, give thanks to the God of heaven!
　　For His mercy endures forever.
　　　(NKJV, emphasis added)

Talk about echoes of mercy!

Mercy is core to who God is. To know God is to know that he is merciful and that he is motivated by his mercy. As a matter of fact, at times, it causes him to act in unseemly ways.

Not long ago, after much procrastination, my wife

and I finalized our wills. We made it a family affair, inviting our six children into the conversation so we could make it a learning experience for all. It was a good teaching moment, and I was proud of them for how seriously they took the conversation. However, I can't imagine how I would react if one of my children, now aware of my last will and testament, came to me and asked for his or her share of the inheritance. I hope I would be slow in speaking an angry word, gracious in my demeanor, loving in my facial expressions, and compassionate with my child. I hope I would be as merciful as the father was with the prodigal son in Luke 15.

One day his youngest son came to him and asked him to divide the inheritance. The son then proceeded to squander it all in wild living. It was only when the money ran out and a severe famine set in that he made his way back home.

Not only did the father humble himself and grant his son's insulting request for an early inheritance, but he also did the unthinkable upon the prodigal's return: "He ran to his son, threw his arms around him and kissed him" (Luke 15:20). Many have pointed out how undignified it was in that culture for a grown man to hike up his robe, bare his legs, and run—let alone the fact that he was running to the one who, in essence, had spat in his face. His early request for his birthright was tantamount to saying, "Father, I wish you were dead."

But mercy is God's grace in action. And in this parable we see God, represented by the father, graciously stooping to a status beneath him. Jesus is very careful to give us the reason for the unseemly behavior of the father. "But while he was still a long way off, his father saw him and was filled with compassion [mercy] for him" (Luke 15:20).

Many parents have experienced the moment when they realize they are embarrassing their children. One day they want to show you off and the next they are asking you to drop them off a block away from school, not to sing in front of their friends, or not to tuck in your shirt because you don't look cool.

Our Father (God) takes embarrassment and humiliation upon himself as he bends from on high, where the train of his robe fills the temple, to be born into the aroma of animals and their feeding trough. That's what the incarnation means. Ultimately he took on "the very nature of a servant, being made in human likeness. And being found in appearance as a man, he humbled himself and became obedient to death—even death on a cross!" (Phil. 2:7–8).

God's willingness to act mercifully echoes throughout his holy Word. Morning by morning, like sound traveling through a canyon, new mercies we discover, and we find new hope. The good news is that God's mercy specifically addresses two of the harshest aspects of human existence: sin and suffering. Mercy presupposes both.

Mercy Assumes We Are Sinners

Many times those who prayed the mercy prayer didn't just say, "Lord, have mercy." No, they ended the most prayed prayer recognizing an essential fact about themselves: "Lord, have mercy on me, *a sinner.*"

Mercy assumes we will sin. Arthur W. Pink said it well when he wrote, "Mercy . . . denotes the ready inclination of God to relieve the misery of fallen creatures. Thus 'mercy' presupposes sin."[4] We are fallen creatures with a propensity for wrongdoing. The result? Shame. Guilt. Strained relationships. Regret.

The good news of God's mercy is that he desires to relieve the consequences of our sin, the worst of which is the toll it exacts on our relationship with him. We were meant to walk with God in the cool of the garden of Eden, and yet, when we sin, we find ourselves hiding from God, blaming those around us, and searching for makeshift fig leaves to cover our shame. God's reflexive response is to lessen these consequences—to show mercy.

When Adam and Eve ate of the one tree that God forbade, the penalty was severe: death and banishment from the garden. Yet God replaced their wilting leaves with something more durable; and as they moved east of Eden, one thing became surprisingly clear: while they had left the garden, God had not left them. His presence served as a balm of hope upon their guilt.

Anyone who's been to Sunday school or watched the Super Bowl knows the verse John 3:16: "For God so loved the world that he gave his one and only Son, that whoever believes in him shall not perish but have eternal life." But the next verse is equally important: "For God did not send his Son into the world to condemn the world, but to save the world through him" (John 3:17). God is not in the condemning business.

If we want to see how Jesus treats sinners, we need to look no further than the woman caught in adultery. Only a few chapters after Christ says that he has not come to condemn us, we see him backing up his words with actions as a woman is mercilessly dragged into his presence. Her accusers informed Jesus that she was caught in the act of sexual sin and that the law said she deserved death. They wanted Jesus to weigh in on her fate. The crime was a serious one, but there was something more sinister at play: "They were using this question as a trap, in order to have a basis for accusing him" (John 8:6). They hoped Jesus would discredit himself with his response and weaken his standing with the people.

Think of the planning that might have gone into this ruse. First, they must have had a meeting about how to trap Jesus, where they hatched a plan starting with catching someone committing a capital crime. We are only left to our imaginations as to how they succeeded in catching this woman. Did they voyeuristically peep through a crack in the curtains while hiding in the bushes? Or did one of them seduce her only to betray her to the authorities? We don't know. What we do know is that they thought this was the best way to trap Jesus. Why? He had a reputation. He was known for mercy. They concocted this plan because they knew, when given the chance, he would seek to remove the penalty for this guilty woman.

Jesus diverted everyone's attention from her naked shame as he knelt down to write something in the dirt. They didn't count on Jesus' brilliant response. He upheld grace and truth by saying, "If any one of you is without sin, let him be the first to throw a stone at her" (John 8:7).

Reluctantly, the crowd of accusers dropped their rocks and dispersed.

Only Jesus was without sin. Only Jesus could justly throw the first stone. Only Jesus remained. She was left standing face-to-face with the only person qualified to carry out her sentence.

"Woman, where are they? Has no one condemned you?" Jesus asked.

"No one, sir," she said.

"Then neither do I condemn you," Jesus declared. "Go now and leave your life of sin" (John 8:10–11).

Mercy assumes we are sinners. Thus the apostle Paul proclaims, "Therefore, there is now no condemnation for those who are in Christ Jesus" (Rom. 8:1). When we allow that to settle into our souls, we will experience true freedom: knowing that God, though he is holy and just, desires to grant us a pardon through Christ. Seeing firsthand how Jesus deals with someone caught in the act should cause us to run to him (not away) despite our sin, for we have nothing to fear.

In his book *Abba's Child: The Cry of the Heart for Intimate Belonging*, Brennan Manning tells a story of when he was a young novice in the Franciscan order. The monks practiced self-flagellation, the beating of oneself (in this case, with a foot-long piece of telephone wire) for the purpose of purifying oneself of sinful desires. On Friday nights during the season of Lent, Psalm 51 was recited aloud by an assigned priest, while they each would go into their monastery cells and beat themselves. Manning whipped his back and buttocks so severely that when his blisters were observed the next day in the showers, he was reprimanded for being too zealous. He wrote, "Truth to tell, I was trying desperately to make myself pleasing to God."

Brother Dismas occupied a neighboring cell to Manning, and Manning could hear the ruthless sound of his self-scourging. Fearing that his brother was also going too far, Manning peeked through a crack in the door only to see Brother Dismas whipping the wall with a cigarette in his hand and a smile on his face. Manning concludes, "I pitied the poor wretch and returned to my cell with an insufferable sense of spiritual superiority."[5]

What is painfully ironic is that this all happened while Psalm 51 was read aloud. The psalm begins,

> Have mercy upon me, O God,
> According to Your lovingkindness;
> According to the multitude of Your tender
>   mercies,
> Blot out my transgressions. (v. 1 NKJV)

Why do we seek to deal with our sin differently than God does? Why do we beat ourselves up because of the things we have done? We are prone to think change happens through discipline and trying harder. But one reason God is not into condemnation is because his goal is transformation—and that happens best in an environment of mercy.

The apostle Paul wrote, "Do not conform any longer to the pattern of this world, but be transformed by the renewing of your mind" (Rom. 12:2). We are called to be transformed, and it is crucial that we understand the setting in which the transformation occurs. Before Paul called us to transformation he said, "Therefore, I urge you, brothers, in view of God's mercy, to offer your bodies as living sacrifices, holy and pleasing to God—this is your spiritual act of worship" (Rom. 12:1). The Christian life is best lived within eyeshot of the loving-kindness of God. Transformation flourishes "in view of God's mercy."

How do we change? Is it by trying harder? Is it out of duty? Fear? While these motivations work in the short run when it comes to keeping our behaviors suppressed, true transformation only happens when we exchange our shame and fear for his mercy. As Steve and Sally Breedlove and Ralph and Jennifer Ennis put it, "The mercy we are offered in Jesus Christ brings forgiveness. But it is more than that; it is also an offer that transforms our very identity—we are invited into the family of God as adopted children. Christians call that identity-level change *transformation*."[6] God's mercy creates the canopy under which our growth into Christlikeness takes root.

True change occurs as we bask in the warmth and comfort of God's compassion and grace. True transformation is brought about not by making commitments that begin with "I am going to . . ." or "I will try harder to . . ." No, any strategy for change that begins with "I" is doomed to fail. True change begins with God. Ultimately, the alteration of our hearts takes place in the hands of a God who is slow to anger and abounding in love. His kindness leads us to repentance (Rom. 2:4). God's mercy is for sinners, and God's mercy is also for those who are in pain.

Mercy Assumes We Are Suffering

Jesus said, "In this world you will have trouble" (John 16:33). Jesus suffered. We will suffer. Pain is going to happen to all of us—to me, to you. Someone you trust is going to break your heart. Your grandmother who raised you is going to die. Divorce will be decreed even though you don't want it. God's mercy assumes we suffer and that we will need ointment on our wounds, whether they are the result of an absentee father or chemotherapy. God makes his mercy present to us in our pain and our sufferings—deserved and undeserved.

Joseph discovered this. Sold by his jealous brothers into slavery and then wrongfully accused of sexual assault against his boss's wife, he was sentenced to do time in the personal prison of the king. Clearly a painful situation. As Joseph began his incarceration as an innocent man, we read this: "But the LORD was with Joseph and showed him mercy." Do you see it? God didn't spare Joseph the pain, but in the midst of the suffering he made his mercy available. The result was that God "gave him favor in the sight of the keeper of the prison" (Gen. 39:21 NKJV).

Sojourner Truth is one of my heroes of the faith. She was born a slave in the late 1700s and given the name Isabella Baumfree. Her owners were a Dutch family in upstate New York and she grew up speaking no English. "Belle," as she was known, was one of thirteen children. Though their owner did not beat them or physically abuse them, the family's living conditions were appalling. Then, upon her original owner's death, she was sold to John Dumont. Life with Dumont was worse, as he whipped her for not understanding English. His wife sexually abused her. Even so, Belle eventually learned English and gained her freedom when slavery was abolished in New York in 1827. In obedience to God, she changed her name to Sojourner Truth and committed herself to traveling the land and telling others about the kingdom of God.

In her autobiography, she tells about finding her mother in tears and asking her why. Her mother answered, "Oh, my child, I am thinking of your brothers and sisters that have been sold away from me."[7] At night, fearing that the rest of her children would experience the same fate, her mother would call the siblings together and teach them, saying, "My children, there is a God, who hears and sees you. . . . and when you are beaten, or cruelly treated, or fall into any trouble, you must ask help of him, and he will always hear and help you."[8] She did not know if God would spare her children from the auction block; but she did know, from personal experience, what to do in the midst of suffering. Thus, Sojourner learned at a young age that God is with us in our darkest hours. She also learned what to do in such circumstances: namely, ask the Lord for help—for mercy.

When the Fugitive Slave Act of 1850 was passed, decreeing that all runaway slaves were to be returned to their owners, Sojourner Truth sat and listened to the great abolitionist Frederick Douglass address a gathering of those troubled by the events. Douglass strayed from his nonviolent convictions and called for Southern slaves to arm themselves and fight. Sojourner Truth, while discouraged by the state of injustice, stood up and asked a penetrating question: "Frederick, is God dead?"[9]

"Is God dead?" is even inscribed on her tombstone, for Sojourner knew a God who was present during painful times in ways that could not be explained. She had endured abuse, beatings, and the helplessness of watching her own son sold illegally across state lines.

Sin's consequences are our reality on earth. This world is broken. The mercy prayer is for the suffering of the world. When we hear of a flood, tornado, or hurricane, we present our plea for mercy on behalf of the victims. The mercy prayer is for those who know God is with them in and through suffering. Every time this request is prayed to Jesus, it is for the alleviation of pain and suffering, not for a lessening of the penalty of sin.

Consider these two parents who came to Jesus with the mercy prayer.

In the gospel of Matthew, we see a father modeling this for us as he sought mercy from Jesus on behalf of his son. He approached Jesus when the disciples were unable to help his son, who was demon-possessed and suffered seizures. The boy's body bore the scars from burns he had received from falling into a fire during one of his episodes. I imagine there were many times when the father thought his son had died as he found him floating in the nearby lake and was able to resuscitate him with his own makeshift version of CPR. So finally, he came to Jesus and fell on his knees with his simple yet desperate request, "Lord, have mercy on my son" (Matt. 17:15).

The Canaanite mother shows us an even deeper truth.

Leaving that place, Jesus withdrew to the region of Tyre and Sidon. A Canaanite woman from that vicinity came to him, crying out, "Lord, Son of David, have mercy on me! My daughter is demon-possessed and suffering terribly." (Matt. 15:21–22)

This was a desperate mother at the end of her rope. She didn't come to Jesus quietly or politely; she shouted to Jesus at the top of her lungs. She was frantic to find help for her daughter. She was coming to Jesus for mercy not because of sin but because of suffering.

We are not told anything beyond the fact that her daughter was demon-possessed. We can only imagine the mental anguish and social ostracism this young girl endured. So this mother's only hope was to get to Jesus. Maybe he could help.

Interestingly, her request was for herself. Certainly she wanted her daughter's suffering lessened, but she specifically said, "Lord, Son of David, have mercy on me!" It was a request for herself. Not only was her daughter suffering but she was as well. Caring for a sick person is itself a form of suffering. It hurts to watch your loved one undergo pain. You do your best, but you feel helpless. Any parent of a special-needs child knows this kind of suffering. You recognize that your child is in worse condition, yet you yourself are exhausted mentally and physically in the caretaker's role. Jesus desires to grant mercy to the merciful (Matt. 5:17).

If you are a nurse, you do much to help others find comfort. You read vitals, administer medication, and listen to patients in their times of need. After a day of giving, your body is exhausted and your mind races through the events of the day; remarkably, you find that you are suffering too.

Or perhaps you are caring for your parents in their latter years of life. It's not easy having tough conversations about selling the family house. It's difficult to tell your dad that he can't drive anymore. Why is it that you are so torn up inside when it's your parents who are going through the loss, not you? Because your heart is like a sponge soaking in the moment. Detachment is nearly impossible and certainly undesirable. You suffer, too, as you lose the parents of your younger years. It is okay to seek relief in your prayers.

I'm thinking of a woman who sits with her invalid son at the hospital. He is unable to speak, hear, or even walk. This little boy's life has been miserable. And so has hers. As she sits there, she reflects on everything she has lost. Her marriage couldn't survive the stress. And with no health insurance and mounting medical bills, she contemplates the unthinkable—*Should I relinquish my parental rights to the state?* That way his care would be covered, and perhaps someone could meet his needs in her place. Anguish. Suffering.

The Canaanite mother was not asking Jesus to help just her daughter; she needed mercy too. This instance of the mercy prayer is no different than all the other pleas for mercy that Christ received: every time someone seeks out Jesus for mercy, he responds. The biblical text says, "Then Jesus answered, 'Woman, you have great faith! Your request is granted.' And her daughter was healed from that very hour" (Matt. 15:28).

Jesus hears the cries of pain and suffering. He takes action.

The Trauma of Temptation

It's important to consider why we sin in the first place, especially since sin and suffering are so closely linked. Theologically speaking, we know it is because we are born into this sin-soaked world and daily face the triple threats of the world, the flesh, and the devil.

Others have pointed out that sin can be a pleasurable experience, and we are pleasure seekers. God "satisfies [our] desires with good things," but so often we aren't willing to wait for the "good things" and settle for lesser things (Ps. 103:5). The inevitable aftermath of sin is shame, and (as we have seen) God makes his mercy available even in these times of self-inflicted trouble.

In either case, we sin because we give in to temptation. But such answers, helpful as they are, can only take us so far. We need to go deeper.

Resisting temptation is a form of suffering. Sin is a relief from this struggle. When we are tempted, we are pummeled by the traitor within (the flesh), bombarded by an aggravating system of messages (the world), and harassed by the accuser (Satan)—sometimes all at once! That is pain and suffering, and thus temptation is a traumatic experience.

The Bible says,

> No temptation has seized you except what is common to man. And God is faithful; he will not let you be tempted beyond what you can bear. But when you are tempted, he will also provide a way out so that you can stand up under it. (1 Cor. 10:13)

Think about some of the words used in that passage to describe what temptation is doing to us and what is required to overcome it.

- *Seized*—to grab on to, to lay hold of, to not let go. Kidnap. Snatch. Hijack. Abduct.

- *Escape*—to run away from danger.
- *Bear* and *stand up under it*—to resist against pressure, to lift something heavy. Endure.

Those are words of struggle and survival. Think about how you would respond to someone if he or she said, "I was walking through the woods and was seized by a wild animal. I was able to escape because I was able to bear the pain of its claws as I threw it off and ran." Or, "At work, a pallet of material fell on top of me. I was seized under its weight. After lying there a while I stood up under the weight and escaped."

What would your response be? "Are you all right?" "Were you injured?" "Did you go to the hospital?" "Were there any broken bones?" "Did you need stitches?"

These are words used to describe a distressing ordeal. Thankfully the text says, "God is faithful; he will not let you be tempted beyond what you can bear." But that doesn't take away from the fact that we have to bear it. Suffer it.

Temptation is a form of trauma, and sustained temptation is sustained suffering. To resist sin day after day is traumatic. Going to battle can take its toll.

I once read an article about hockey enforcers. These are the guys who do all the fighting. In hockey, there is an unwritten rule that says, "Don't lay a hand on our good players and high scorers. If you do, then you will get punched in the face by our enforcer." The article talked about how difficult it is for these paid brawlers to wake up each day knowing that their job is to hit and be hit. Just the anticipation of the battle is traumatic. Those on the front lines in the military know this kind of anxiety all too well. That is why it is important that they receive care for the ravages of war and the post-traumatic stress that ensues.

Spiritually speaking, fighting sin takes its toll too. To resist sin is to suffer. There is no other way to describe the feeling—the ordeal—brought about by temptation. Oftentimes we choose to sin because we want the suffering to end. We know God has promised to provide a way out and in the meantime we are supposed to be able to bear it. But sometimes the weight feels too heavy. That is precisely the time when we need to cry out to God with the mercy prayer.

As Christians, we have chosen to fight sin. What most of us don't know is that to seek victory over sin is to choose to suffer. We've discussed how Christ makes his mercy available to us during all kinds of suffering. This also includes the suffering associated with temptation. That means that not only does God desire to help us after we sin, but before as well.

Jesus wants us to seek him when we are actually

being tempted. Our natural inclination is to isolate ourselves when we are contemplating wrong, yet Christ desires to be invited into that part of our lives, for he knows what it feels like to be tempted.

Let these words about Jesus wash over your soul: "Because he himself suffered when he was tempted, he is able to help those who are being tempted" (Heb. 2:18). Don't miss that. Jesus "suffered when he was tempted."

When we think of the suffering of Jesus, we usually limit it to the physical pain that surrounded the crucifixion. We think of the lack of sleep and the scourging; the loss of blood and carrying the weight of the rough wood; the nails and hanging helplessly. But according to this verse, Jesus' suffering started before the cross— "when he was tempted."

Immediately I think of Jesus in the desert and the Garden of Gethsemane (Matt. 4:1–11; 26:36–56). In the desert, Jesus was seized by Satan's offers. In the garden, on the night of his arrest, we see him cry out under the stress. In both cases he did not sin, but he did suffer. And these weren't his only moments of temptation. Later on in Hebrews we read that Jesus was "tempted in every way, just as we are—yet was without sin" (Heb. 4:15).

Do you have a besetting temptation? Is there something that is outside of God's will that you fight every day? Listen to this remarkable truth: Jesus personally knows the pain of persisting against that sin—your specific sin. Thus, he also knows how to alleviate your specific ache. Wait for him.

The mercy prayer is not just for those who want relief from the consequences of their sins. It is also for those who are in pain, whether it is emotional or physical. "Lord, have mercy" is the prayer we offer to God as we are tempted to walk away from him and to dive into sin. It is the heart cry of those who know the pain of temptation.

As a matter of fact, ever since Jesus made the mercy prayer the most answered prayer, whole communities have devoted themselves to seeking God for mercy. The oldest Christian monasteries in the world can be found in the Egyptian desert, and for some seventeen centuries people have lived in these places for the purpose of organizing their lives around the mercy prayer. The prayer books of Lutheran, Catholic, Anglican, and Presbyterian congregations are loaded with litanies containing the mercy prayer. The old saint who sits in the front row of her Baptist church is known to whisper the mercy prayer with tears in her eyes as her pastor tells the congregation about another incident of gang violence in their community. We join with them and can even learn to pray it with every beat of our hearts. Those who have gone before us tell us that when we do this we will learn the meaning of, "I sleep, but my heart is awake" (Song 5:2 NKJV).

THREE

The Prayer of the Heart

What if, "Lord, have mercy" was not only the most prayed prayer in the Bible but in your life as well? Many Christians through the ages believed that this should be the case.

We have so much to learn from Christians who are different than us. I grew up as a Southern Baptist. Then I spent eight wonderful years in a Presbyterian church. Today, I'm the pastor of an independent, inter-denominational church. We aren't officially associated with any particular denomination not because we believe the denominations are bad; rather, we desire to look back over the last two thousand years and see what we have to learn from all the different groups of people that have followed Christ. The different labels—Baptist, Presbyterian, Pentecostal, Lutheran, Episcopal, Catholic, and the list goes on—simply represent the variety of ways and approaches others have taken in following Jesus.

I love being part of a community that doesn't ask people to leave their denominations at the door. If you grew up Baptist, then we say, come to our church and be Baptist. Or if you grew up Presbyterian, be Presbyterian. We want to see what happens when all these different traditions of following Jesus Christ commit to worshipping together in one place, honoring and celebrating our differences. It's a beautiful thing!

The Closer We Get to God

One denomination has majored on the mercy of God: the Eastern Orthodox church. For almost two thousand years this segment of Christianity has made the mercy of God central to their understanding of the meaning of following Jesus—especially when it comes to prayer. They recognize that Daniel was right when he prayed, "We do not make requests of you because we are righteous, but because of your great mercy" (Dan. 9:18).

The Eastern Orthodox church is rather unknown to most Western Christians. These followers of Jesus are mostly located in Russia, Greece, the Middle East, and Africa. When it comes to understanding the most prayed prayer, we would do well to learn from them.

Their theologians first recognized our tendency to pray for God's mercy. They were the ones to remark on how common it was for the people of God to cry out to him for mercy in the Psalms:

> Answer me when I call to you,
>> O my righteous God.
> Give me relief from my distress;
>> be merciful to me and hear my prayer.
>
> (Ps. 4:1)

> Be merciful to me, LORD, for I am faint;
>> O LORD, heal me, for my bones are in
>> agony.
>
> (Ps. 6:2)

> O LORD, see how my enemies persecute me!
>> Have mercy and lift me up from the gates
>> of death.
>
> (Ps. 9:13)

Hear my cry for mercy
    as I call to you for help,
as I lift up my hands toward your Most Holy
    Place.

(Ps. 28:2)

To you, O Lord, I called;
    to the Lord I cried for mercy.

(Ps. 30:8)

It was also the Orthodox that noticed that the one sentence spoken to Jesus more than any other was, "*Kyrie eleison.*" This branch of Christianity pointed out that all of us are in a line leading to God's courtroom, and we all have one hope in that setting: that God is merciful.

They even began to ask, could it be that the closer you get to God the more you pray the mercy prayer? What if our closeness to Christ actually *increases* the frequency of our requests for his mercy?

We normally think the opposite—something like this: *I was living a really bad life and was in need of mercy. But once I embraced Jesus and asked him into my heart, he took the burden of sin off of me. Now I can leave behind the consequences of my sin, move on, and grow closer to God.*

Eastern Orthodox believers say the opposite is true.

Our recognition of our need for mercy only intensifies the closer we get to God. It's as if the cross awakens our appetite for his compassion. We actually desire God's mercy more the closer we get to him, not only because we see our shortcomings in light of his perfection but also because knowing God is knowing that he is merciful. This is a lesson we can see illustrated in the tabernacle found in the Old Testament.

The architecture of this ancient worship space communicated the spiritual life in tangible reality. As worshippers walked into the tabernacle, they saw a large courtyard with a number of furnishings signifying different aspects of knowing God. The large basin of water represented cleansing. Burning incense signified the prayers of God's people. Furthest away from the entrance, deepest within the tabernacle, was the Holy of Holies. To enter that space was to enter the presence of God. The closer one was to this most holy place, the closer one was to God's glory. Very few people were actually allowed to enter this sacred room. But if you were to go in beyond the veil and enter, you would see the ark of the covenant—the throne of God. What was the name given to the throne? The mercy seat!

The closer you get to God, the more you see his mercy. God is most merciful, and the more we see of him, the more mercy we desire.

With Every Beat of Our Hearts

The most answered prayer has often been called the prayer of the heart. As the Eastern Orthodox church sought to turn the prayer into a way of life, they discovered it is possible to know it by heart—literally. They say it's possible to pray "Lord, have mercy" with every heartbeat.

Try it.

Tonight, when you lay your head down on your pillow, as the sounds of the day begin to fade and your body begins to settle, you'll reach a point of quietness in which you can actually hear and feel your heart beating. You can begin to pray the mercy prayer in rhythm with your heart.

Lord, Jesus, Son of God, have mercy on me.
Lord, Jesus, Son of God, have mercy on me.
Lord, Jesus, Son of God, have mercy on me.

If you do this, you will find that you will continue praying in your sleep. Throughout the night, your subconscious will still seek God. And when you stir, *Kyrie eleison* will be your first waking thought.

With practice, we can build the mercy prayer into our biology. As our hearts pump our lifeblood through our bodies, our spirits will proclaim with each pulse, his "love [mercy] is better than life" (Ps. 63:3 NKJV). Someday our hearts will stop, but his mercies will never cease; for our God always has been and forever will be a compassionate, gracious God, slow to anger and abounding in loving-kindness.

If we were to seek mercy with every beat of our hearts, that would be over a hundred thousand requests every day! Imagine the response.

So why would we want to pray for mercy that much? Doesn't *every* heartbeat sound just a little excessive? As one who has made the mercy prayer my most prayed prayer, I've learned that it's difficult to receive mercy multiple times. No one wants to be a repeat offender; and yet, as hard as it is to admit, that is exactly what we are.

We all have made our promises to God: "Okay, God. I love you and I've done things I shouldn't have. I repent. Now I'm going to walk in the path of the kingdom for real. Have mercy on me! Thank you so much for not doling out the consequences of my sin. I'm now going to walk in your ways." But then we go right out and fall back into the habits and activities we just swore off.

We are so sinful. Unloving. Prideful. We find ourselves coming back to God sooner than we like to admit. We've heard he's the God of second chances, but we're wondering what happens when you've used your second chance three, four, or five times ago. Pride is what keeps us from coming to him again. Pride keeps us from saying, "I've messed up again," and pride is what keeps us far from him.

But because of God's mercy, instead of saying he's the God of second chances, it's more accurate to say that he's the God of *another* chance.

A. W. Tozer points out in his book *The Knowledge of the Holy* that God's mercy is "infinite and inexhaustible." We can never use it up or come to the bottom of the jar. He goes on to say,

> If we could remember that the divine mercy is not a temporary mood but an attribute of God's eternal being, we would no longer fear that it will someday cease to be. Mercy never began to be, but from eternity was; so it will never cease to be. It will never be more since it is itself infinite; and it will never be less because the infinite cannot suffer diminution. Nothing that has occurred or will occur in heaven or earth or hell can change the tender mercies of our God. Forever His mercy stands, a boundless, overwhelming immensity of divine pity and compassion.[1]

Mind-boggling!

Asking for mercy is not about us; it's about God. It is not about admitting who we are but admitting who

God is. Praying often for mercy and making the most answered prayer a way of life is to choose to put God on display in all his glory. Again, Tozer says it so eloquently:

> Were there no guilt in the world, no pain and no tears, God would yet be infinitely merciful; but His mercy might well remain hidden in His heart, unknown to the created universe. No voice would be raised to celebrate the mercy of which none felt the need. It is human misery and sin that call forth the divine mercy.[2]

Praying the mercy prayer gives God another chance to show us he's not a lightning-bolt God. It gives God another opportunity to show he's not the angry, wrathful God that so many have made him out to be.

It's about letting the world see our God for who he really is.

It's not about us; it's about God.

Vain Repetition?

The mercy prayer is not about manipulating God. Nor is it merely a formula. It's much deeper than that, for ultimately all prayer is about interacting with God as we share the desires of our hearts and listen for his. When we ask God for mercy, we are simply responding to what he has already said he wants to do. This is, by the way, the essence of praying in Jesus' name.

Like many Christians, I oftentimes end my prayers, "in Jesus' name, amen." We don't do this because we think it obligates God to answer our prayers. Rather, it is a way of saying that what we have requested is something we think Jesus would be okay having his name attached to. In other words, to pray in the name of Jesus means we are presenting to God something we think Jesus would endorse—something that aligns with his character and will. This confidence comes with knowing who Christ is and what his heart desires.

It was Jesus who said, "I tell you the truth, my Father will give you whatever you ask in my name" (John 16:23). When Jesus said this, his listeners understood that he wasn't advocating just saying the words *in the name of Jesus* in hopes of ingratiating ourselves to God. As a matter of fact, you can pray in Jesus' name without even saying those exact words. The Lord's Prayer is a great example; it clearly represents God's heart, but doesn't end with the words *in Jesus' name.*

"Lord, have mercy" is a prayer close to the heart of Jesus. It's not about coercing God but about recognizing what God already desires to do. I've heard it put this way: "Prayer is not overcoming God's reluctance, but laying hold of His willingness."[3] God has clearly communicated that he wants to pour out his mercy upon us. The most answered prayer aligns our hearts with God's.

It is good to distinguish this kind of praying from the kind Jesus warned about when he said, "When you pray, do not use vain repetitions as the heathen do. For they think that they will be heard for their many words" (Matt. 6:7 NKJV). Notice that Jesus is not against repetition in general but "*vain* repetition" in particular.

There is nothing wrong with repetition in and of itself. A tennis player repeats backhands and a guitarist repeats a scale all with the hopes of getting better. We repetitively do sit-ups and push-ups in order to get stronger. In the Bible, there are many examples of God's people repeating things to him. I've already pointed out that Israel sang "For his mercy endures forever" twenty-six times in Psalm 136. In the Sermon on the Mount, which took place right after Jesus spoke out against vain repetition, he taught us we should pray the Lord's Prayer. He doesn't expect us to only pray this prayer one time and then be done with it; rather, we should pray it often. There is repetition in heaven as well. We are also told about the four living creatures in God's throne room, and "Day and night they never stop saying: 'Holy, holy, holy is the Lord God Almighty, who was, and is, and is to come'" (Rev. 4:8).

The kind of repetition that we should guard against is the kind that can be described as vain—meaningless or mindless. Whether with the prayers we pray before our meals or the ones we use when we tuck in our children, we should make sure we are not just going through the motions. This is true of the mercy prayer as well. But the danger of mindless repetition needn't keep us from pursuing its promise in our lives.

Kyrie eleison. Christe eleison. Kyrie eleison.

FOUR

When You're in Need

F ar and away, King David exceeded everybody else in praying the mercy prayer. This probably shouldn't surprise us, for David understood God's heart. God said so himself: "[God] testified concerning him: 'I have found David son of Jesse a man after my own heart; he will do everything I want him to do'" (Acts 13:22).

When we think of testifying in this sense, it's usually when a person wants to celebrate the goodness of God. The pastor asks, "Can I get a witness?" We say, "I want to testify to God's goodness in my life," or "I want to give testimony about how God's grace has changed my life." When it came to David, though, God essentially said, "I want to raise my right hand and promise to tell the truth about my servant David."

God announced that he had "found David" a man after his heart. Did you know God was searching? We are told that God is searching the earth looking for hearts turned toward him (2 Chron. 16:9). God found such a heart in David.

So what does such a significant person pray? "Lord, have mercy!" David was a man who suffered and sinned much, and, as the record shows, he never hesitated to ask for mercy.

For example, in Psalm 57:1 David prayed, "Have mercy on me, O God, have mercy on me, for in you my soul takes refuge. I will take refuge in the shadow of your wings until the disaster has passed." Right there, two times in the first verse, David pleads for mercy.

Then, get this: "I will take refuge in the shadow of your wings." At first this appears to be a metaphor. God will protect us like a mother bird; and as a mother bird spreads out her wings to shield her youngsters, so God spreads out his love over us, cares for us, and shelters us. There are passages of Scripture that speak of God in this way,[1] but I think David's referring to something else.

When David says, "I will take refuge in the shadow of your wings," I think he's imagining the ark of the covenant, that sacred box where the promises of God were stored. A golden slab served as the lid of the ark. On each side of the ark of the covenant were placed golden angels who spread their wings over that gold slab—that place known as the mercy seat. What a place to take refuge.

When Disaster Strikes

David pleaded, "Have mercy on me, O God, have mercy on me . . . I will [find safety] in the shadow of your wings." I think he was saying, "If I can get to your mercy, that place represented by the ark beneath the shadow of the wings, then everything will be okay." And his need for mercy was urgent. At the end of verse 1 he told us his reasons for this prayer: he was in the midst of disaster.

We so often turn on the TV and discover another major terrorist attack has occurred or another bridge has collapsed and more families are going through catastrophic pain. When disaster knocks, we desperately need mercy to walk in the door.

Peggy was pregnant with her fifth child when they discovered that her husband had cancer. Two and a half years later he died. How does she, a single mom, parent five children? She's trying to figure out, *What do I do when disaster strikes?*

Fortunately for her, during her time of disaster, she had many people who came to her aid. Her boss said, "You know what? I'm going to give you an indefinite sabbatical. You take as much time as you need. I will save your job for you." There was a couple in her church who wrote her a major check and said, "You should not have to worry about money in the midst of disaster, so here's money. May this take away at least some of your worries." Someone gave her a tape titled "God's Plan for Your Future." The title alone gave her hope.[2]

When Your Helpers Hurt

In difficult times, God's mercy can come through those around us. But then there's this question: What happens when disaster strikes your life and the people around you are causing you more pain than the disaster itself? That's what happened in David's life. He was praying for mercy not just because of the disaster but also because of the people who were trying to help him. Look at verse 4 of Psalm 57: "I am in the midst of lions; I lie among ravenous beasts—men whose teeth are spears and arrows, whose tongues are sharp swords." He says essentially, "The people trying to help me are actually hurting me during this difficult time."

What's going on? What's the story behind this?

The wonderful thing about many of David's pleas for mercy is that we're given hints that lead us to the background story. When you turn to Psalm 57 in the NIV version of the Bible, there is a heading: "For the director of music. [To the tune of] 'Do Not Destroy.' Of David. A *miktam*. When he had fled from Saul into the cave." This points us to the full story found in 1 Samuel 22:

> David left Gath and escaped to the cave of Adullam. When his brothers and his father's household heard about it, they went down to him there. All those who were in distress or in debt or discontented gathered around him, and he became their leader. About four hundred men were with him. (vv. 1–2)

Saul was trying to kill him, so David hid in a cave. His family and friends heard about his plight and came to his aid. This is good news, right?

After their arrival, he had four hundred people in this cave with him. He should have been receiving support, but these turned out to be the people he was talking about when he said, "I lie among ravenous beasts . . . whose teeth are spears and arrows, whose tongues are sharp swords." Their words that should have brought comfort were like needles to his soul. The people who should have brought relief only increased his pain. We aren't told exactly what they were saying and doing to hurt David, but either by their bad attitudes or because of their whining and complaining they made his life miserable.

"Lord, have mercy on us" when it's those closest to us whom we fear! Where do we turn when our own inner circle is increasing the pain in our lives?

We don't expect it to be the person we stood with face-to-face at the altar when we said, "For better, for worse, for richer, for poorer, in sickness and in health, forsaking all others, I will keep myself only for you as long as we both shall live," and then walked out of the church seeking to live the fantasy, "happily ever after." But there is a great need for God's mercy for the one who realizes his or her spouse, the one closest to them, has chosen to cause them more pain than anybody else.

Or there's the childhood friend who says, "Why don't we just quit our jobs and go into business together? We might not make more money, but at least we'll be our own bosses and be able to take care of our families." You shake on it and move forward with the business, only to discover years later that your partner was stealing from you, leading to bankruptcy and foreclosure.

What to do in these situations, when one is helpless against these circumstances? David, a man after God's heart, never hesitated to ask God for mercy when his helpers caused hurt in his life.

When We Are Afraid

In 1 Samuel 21, the Bible tells of another incident in the life of David before his family joined him in the cave. "That day David fled from Saul and went to Achish king of Gath." (The place, Gath, is important.)

> But the servants of Achish said to him, "Isn't this David, the king of the land? Isn't he the one they sing about in their dances: 'Saul has slain his thousands, and David his tens of thousands'?"
>
> David took these words to heart and was very much afraid of Achish king of Gath. So he pretended to be insane in their presence; and while he was in their hands he acted like a madman, making marks on the doors of the gate and letting saliva run down his beard. (vv. 10–13)

Fear will cause us to go places we normally wouldn't go. Fear will cause us to do things we never could have pictured ourselves doing.

David was terrified. Saul wanted to kill him. Remember the mighty warrior who even as a small boy went out on a battlefield where no one else dared venture? Nobody would fight Goliath, but then David said essentially, "I'll fight him. He's speaking against the Lord's army."[3] He went out there with a sling and some stones and knocked Goliath out cold. Then he retrieved the giant's sword, hefted its mighty weight in the air, and lopped off Goliath's head. He stood there before the Philistine army, their champion decapitated at his feet, and he displayed his victory. *Bravery* doesn't even seem to be an adequate word.

But just a few years later, he was scared half to death, running from Saul. Where did he run? Gath. Why does that sound familiar? Goliath was from Gath. He went to Goliath's hometown. How insane is that? You have killed their number one warrior and now you say, *I know! I'm going to go seek refuge in the hometown of the enemy.* How terrified must David have been to consider Goliath's hometown safe?

To make matters worse, he was carrying Goliath's sword with him as he waltzed into the giant's hometown (1 Sam. 21:9). Goliath's family was there. The king of the Philistines was there.

They said, "Isn't this David? Isn't this the one who has killed tens of thousands of our people? Why is *he* here?" At that moment he realized fear will cause you to go places you shouldn't go; and once you get there, you wish you hadn't been as afraid.

He ran from fear to fear. Terrified of the circumstances, he chose a novel defense mechanism. He reasoned, *Maybe they won't kill me if they think I'm crazy.* So he decided to act like a madman. He started scratching on the posts like an animal and drooling. With saliva dripping down his beard, he thought to himself, *Now they won't kill me.*

As I said, when fear rules your life, you'll find yourself doing things you never could have pictured yourself doing.

Sharon works for a major university and is the author of many books, but she hasn't always been that way. There was a time when panic and fear ruled her life. When she was invited to her high school prom, she wanted to go, but she chose not to because she was afraid what others would think about her dress and how she danced. In college, she earned a lucrative internship at a local newspaper only to turn it down because she was afraid she couldn't do the job. At the age of thirty, her doctor informed her that a valve on her heart wasn't operating correctly. It wasn't life threatening; she was going to survive, yet her panic attacks increased because every day she wondered, *What would happen if my heart stopped?* Every single day she was afraid of dying, and panic set in.

Fear can paralyze a life. Fear can cause us to roll up in a ball and do nothing. Fear will cause us to do crazy things.

Sharon knew she desperately needed help. She went to holistic healers. She said as she sat in the room with the smells and the bells and the needles in her back, everything was fine, but as soon they took the needles out and she walked away, the panic returned.

She went to a hypnotist and spent hundreds of dollars being hypnotized, trying to get rid of her fear. It didn't work either, but she was still out the money.

She went to a medical doctor. She said the doctor prescribed her medication and her fear subsided, but she was no longer thinking straight.

She was at the end of her rope. What was she supposed to do with all this fear?

"When an answer seemed nowhere in sight," she says, "I decided to turn to the Lord."[4]

When we are paralyzed by fear, when we're out of money, when we're losing hope, there's still something we can do. David showed us. David asked God.

Let me walk you through Psalm 34. As before, notice the heading in the NIV version of the Bible: "Of David. When he pretended to be insane before

Abimelech, who drove him away, and he left." This is during that period of feigned madness we just discussed.

What did he do to get out of these circumstances? "I sought the Lord," he said in verse 4, "and he answered me; he delivered me from all my fears." Did you see the transformation happen? He said, "I once was afraid, but I've been delivered from those fears that were paralyzing me."

There is an important dynamic at play here, and it becomes apparent in the subsequent verses. Verse 7: "The angel of the Lord encamps around those who fear him." Verse 9: "Fear the Lord, you his saints, for those who fear him lack nothing." Verse 11: "Come, my children, listen to me; I will teach you the fear of the Lord."

The fear of the Lord is not the same as the fear of man. Jesus taught us to fear God, not our fellow human beings (Luke 12:4–5). For as the Scriptures say, "The fear of the Lord is the beginning of knowledge" (Prov. 1:7). To fear the Lord means we understand who he is in light of who we are. Our God is awesome and awe-inspiring. In his presence we can't help but love and simultaneously respect his majesty and power. David had discovered an adoring reverence for God.

So we see a transition, a transformation taking place

in David's life. He was petrified of the people around him, and that fear was paralyzing him. Then he owned the fear of God—the true, right fear of God—and that fear turned to praise. It all happened because of the action described in verse 4: "I sought the LORD."

Don't you wonder what he did when he sought the Lord? What did he say to God in the midst of the foaming at the mouth and pretented craziness? What did he pray late at night when he was trying to figure out what to do? Thankfully David wrote down that prayer—the prayer that transformed his life.

As before, the heading of Psalm 56 in the NIV tells us where we are in the story. "For the director of music. To the tune of 'A Dove on Distant Oaks.' Of David. A *miktam*. When the Philistines had seized him in Gath." And what did David pray when the Philistines had seized him at Gath? "Be merciful to me, O God," verse 1 begins, "for men hotly pursue me; all day long they press their attack." He prayed the mercy prayer.

We can pray it not only when those close to us are causing us pain; it's a prayer we also can pray when we are afraid. Lord, have mercy when our fear is taking us places we don't want to go. Lord, have mercy on us when our fear is leading us to do things we never could have pictured ourselves doing.

- Lord, have mercy on us when our insecurities have us so afraid that people will see us for who we really are that we put up facades so people will think better of us.
- Lord, have mercy on us when we buy houses that are too big and cars that are too luxurious and clothes that are too nice, and end up sitting in our living rooms with piles of bills and debt, never sure if we can answer the phone and hear a friendly voice instead of the creditor.
- Lord, have mercy on the young teen whose crime was so heinous that he was tried as an adult. He now sits in his prison cell staring at the walls and the reality of his future.
- Lord, have mercy upon victims of crime and those diagnosed with cancer.
- Lord, have mercy upon those just admitted into hospice care and those who stand around their bedsides.
- Lord, have mercy when fear drives us to places we shouldn't go, and we are doing things we shouldn't do.
- Lord, have mercy.

I promise you, if you ask him for mercy, he will never turn you away.

When We Do Things We Shouldn't

Not all of us have people in our lives causing us a disabling fear or pain, but "all have sinned and fall short of the glory of God" (Rom. 3:23). In light of God's justice, we need mercy when we say, "If God gave me what I deserve for the sins I've committed, I could not survive."

At the beginning of Psalm 51 the heading in the NIV version of the Bible reads, "For the director of music. A psalm of David. When the prophet Nathan came to him after David had committed adultery with Bathsheba."

David was at home at a time when kings were supposed to be off at war. He was at home, bored, and standing on his palatial roof. He looked down and he saw Bathsheba taking a bath. He had her come to his house, and one thing led to another. Then David found out Bathsheba was pregnant. What did he do? He sent her husband, a soldier in David's army, to the front line of the battlefield, the place of greatest danger. Then a clandestine, orchestrated murder took place. On David's orders, the rest of the men pulled back, leaving Bathsheba's husband unprotected. He was killed, as David had hoped, to hide the adultery. Sin upon sin.

But sin doesn't hide. The prophet Nathan confronted David about his wrongs, and David, faced with the evil he had committed, repented.

Given the backstory, how else could the psalm begin except with the mercy prayer?

Have mercy on me, O God,
    according to your unfailing love;
according to your great compassion
    blot out my transgressions.

(Ps. 51:1)

Grace is receiving what we don't deserve. But before we can receive what we don't deserve, God must first refrain from giving us what we *do* deserve. Mercy carves a path for God's grace.

But you might say, "I'm not an adulterer." You might say, "I'm not a murderer." You might also say that you are those things. If so, take heart: God's mercy is available to you, just as it was to David. But before the rest of us are so quick to distance ourselves from David, let's pause. The more I've studied the life of David, the more I see myself in him in ways I wish I didn't. There have been times when I knew I was supposed to be doing the right thing, but instead I did my own thing and put myself in a situation where I was open to temptation. How about you? Have there been times when you were supposed to be one place, and because you weren't you opened yourself up to the wrong things? We *are* like David.

Have you ever misused power? Whatever your place in life, you have some authority and some power you could use for good. You have prestige; you have position. Do you think Bathsheba really had a choice about whether to go over to the palace that day? When the king says, "Come to my house," can you say, "No, thank you"? Bathsheba *had* to go. Have you ever misused power to gratify your own desires? Lord, have mercy on us when we do.

What about contentment? This may not make sense in our culture, but it was true in David's. If you were the king, not only did you have your wife but you also had concubines. Concubines were the king's prostitutes, so to speak—women who weren't really wives but were available for sex. If you study the life of David and the kings, there were many (perhaps hundreds) in the king's concubine group.[5] If he didn't want to go be with his wife, he could go be with the concubines. On that day or night when he stood up on his roof, David had many options available to him, yet he wanted what he didn't have. Can you relate? Perhaps you're not content with what God has provided—not content with the plenty that you have. If that describes you, Lord, have mercy. In the words of David,

> [Lord, have mercy on us]
> > according to your unfailing love;
> according to your great compassion
> > blot out [our] transgressions.
> Wash away all [our] iniquity
> > and cleanse [us] from [our] sin.

> (Ps. 51:1–2)

That's why Psalm 51 is one of the most beloved psalms. That's why many of us have underlined almost all of it. It's why so many Bibles flop to Psalm 51 when we let them fall open; for we know our sin, and what we need is God's mercy.

What the Cross Is All About

In the last chapter I told you that the Eastern Orthodox church has spent a lot of time trying to incorporate the mercy of God into their faith and practice. They are devoted to understanding how to pray, *"Kyrie eleison*—Lord, have mercy." Have you ever seen an

Eastern Orthodox cross? It looks a little different than the ones we normally wear around our necks or see in our Western churches.

It's called a three-bar cross. You can see the basic parts of the cross where Christ's arms were stretched out and where his body was. The short line on the top represents the sign that was above his head: "THIS IS JESUS, THE KING OF THE JEWS."[6] Then there is that odd line, the diagonal line across the long vertical one. What's that about? Eastern Orthodox Christians use it as a reminder of the mercy of God. When Christ hung on the cross, there was a thief on his right and a thief on his left—one who repented and received mercy and one who didn't.

These men were guilty as charged, and obviously in a place they didn't want to be. They had done things they shouldn't have done. Those around them were harming them. They were afraid and dying. What did the thieves need? Mercy.

Were they sinning against God? They were spitting at Jesus, they were taunting him, and they were cussing at him, yet what happened? One turned to Jesus and one didn't. One went to a place we don't like to talk about, and to the other one Jesus said, "Today you will be with me in paradise," because his mercy is available to all (Luke 23:43).

If fear is driving your life, seek his mercy. If friends are causing you pain, seek his mercy. If the things you've done and the things you shouldn't have done are ever before you, seek his mercy.

His mercy will transform. If you ask, just as David did, you will discover that he will cleanse, restore, and renew you. Ask him—in the name of Jesus—ask him.

FIVE

Nothing Less than a Miracle

The Bible tells a story about men who have only heard about Jesus, but haven't actually seen him:

> As Jesus went on from there, two blind men followed him, calling out, "Have mercy on us, Son of David!"
>
> When he had gone indoors, the blind men came to him, and he asked them, "Do you believe that I am able to do this?"
>
> "Yes, Lord," they replied.
>
> Then he touched their eyes and said, "According to your faith will it be done to you"; and their sight

was restored. Jesus warned them sternly, "See that no one knows about this." But they went out and spread the news about him all over that region. (Matt. 9:27–31)

Try to picture it. Two blind men following Jesus. How did they do this? Did they use makeshift canes to help them feel their way down the street and through the crowd? Did they listen for his voice, adjusting their courses every time they heard him say something? Did they ever lose him because he turned a corner, forcing them to desperately ask bystanders, "Which way did he go?" in order to be steered in the right direction? Did they link arms and feel their way down the streets and the buildings?

Somehow these two men followed Jesus though they couldn't see where he was or where he was going. They persisted because, while they couldn't see him, they had heard about the things he had done in the lives of others.

They overheard whispers about a woman who had a menstrual flow that would not stop for over a decade of her life, which had reduced her to a shell of a woman by the time she met Jesus, socially outcast, physically and financially depleted. She merely touched the corner of his garment, and Jesus healed her.

They heard about this girl who was cold dead, and Jesus went to her house and raised her to life again.

"News of this spread through all that region," say the Scriptures, and no wonder (Matt. 9:26).

While they had not seen Jesus, they had heard about what he could do, and now they were following him by faith and not by sight. Their request was simple: "Have mercy on us, Son of David!" There it is again: the most asked and most answered prayer. As they tracked and trailed him, they kept saying, "Have mercy on us, Son of David! Have mercy on us, Son of David!"

Did you catch that? They knew who he was: the Son of David. That's the title given to the Messiah in the Old Testament. The one who would come from the line of David. The one who would sit on the throne of David. The one who would rule forever. Son of David: the Messiah, the Anointed One. This was the one they had been waiting for. The prophets had spoken of him.

My guess is they knew what the Messiah was supposed to do. While they may not have been able to read the Old Testament themselves, they must have heard it read. There was one passage about the Messiah that they probably memorized. It's found in Isaiah 35, and it speaks of what the Son of David was supposed to do when he arrived.

Strengthen the feeble hands, steady the knees that give way; say to those with fearful hearts, "Be strong,

do not fear; your God will come, he will come with
vengeance; with divine retribution he will come to
save you." Then will the eyes of the blind be opened.
(vv. 3–5)

The Son of David opens eyes. I think they knew
about this prophecy. And now there he was—about to
pass them by. They couldn't see him, but they desired
to, and so they followed.

"Son of David, have mercy on us. Son of David,
have mercy on us."

Do You Believe?

It doesn't seem appropriate to say that Jesus was ignor-
ing them, but he wasn't responding to them either. He
must have been able to hear them cry, "Have mercy on
us. Have mercy on us," but it appears as if Jesus just kept
walking. It wasn't until these two men followed him
indoors that he engaged them in conversation.

Why did Jesus wait until they were inside? One
author wrote these insightful words:

It is all very well to take a decision for Jesus on the
flood tide of emotion at some great gathering, or in
some little group charged with spiritual power. But

after the crowd a man must go home and be alone . . .
what really matters most is not what a man does in
the crowd, but what he does when he is alone with
Christ. Jesus compelled these men to face him alone.[1]

It's one thing to be faithful at church where everyone is singing songs and carrying their Bibles, but it's
another thing to follow him when nobody is looking.
Maybe that's why Jesus wanted them away from the
crowd. He wanted to hear what they truly desired. So
he asked them a rather odd question: "Do you believe
that I am able to do this?" (Matt. 9:28).

Believe what? That he can be merciful? Why do we
need to have faith for God to have mercy on us? What is
so hard about believing God is compassionate and gracious, slow to anger, and abounding in love? Why would
he ask, "Do you believe that I am able to do this?" All
they wanted was mercy, right?

This passage taught me that my view of mercy was
far too small. When I asked God for mercy, I acted as
though I was just asking for charity. As if I'm a beggar
on the side of the road, and God is just a wealthy person
with a lot of money; all I'm asking is for him to just flip
me some spare change. But asking for mercy is not just
asking for God to be charitable or extra nice to us. It is
so much more than that.

When Jesus said, "Do you believe I am able to do this for you?" he was pointing out the true nature of mercy: to request mercy from God is to request nothing less than a miracle. When we say, "Lord, have mercy," we are asking God to intervene in our lives. We are asking God to step in, look at our situation, and supernaturally intrude upon our circumstances and change the course of our lives. That's God's mercy.

This kind of mercy is much more than him merely deciding to give us a free pass. Think of it this way: imagine a line of dominoes. You push over the first one, and then you see the consequences; it hits another, which hits another, and so on. We say, "Lord, have mercy," and what we mean is, "Down the road somewhere, step in. Pull a domino out so this chain of events that I have started will cease. Have mercy on me. Step in. Do something about this."

It is God stopping something in our lives that otherwise would naturally occur. It is a supernatural intervention so that the normal, expected, deserved course of events doesn't happen. It's a miracle.

Kyrie eleison is the number one prayer of people who have sinned. When we sin, we must face the chain of events we have caused. We see the pain that is now coming into our lives and the lives of others; we feel the weight of our guilt and regret and we say, "Lord, have mercy."

What we're saying is, "Can you alleviate the pain? Can you alleviate the guilt? Can you not make me experience what I'm supposed to experience right now? I need you to suspend the natural consequences. I need a miracle."

It's like a young woman, scared and conflicted, showing up at the abortion clinic only to find out that she is not pregnant. Even more so, it's like asking your employer for forgiveness after you've been caught embezzling and *also* asking that your boss would have a change of heart and let you keep your job in spite of your wrong actions. It's like a teenager asking to go to the movies with her friends right after she's been grounded for breaking curfew.

There are consequences to our sin. Sin is the trigger that sends the domino train racing. When we seek mercy from God—"God, have mercy on me. Do something with the consequences"—we are asking him to stop the chain of events that we have set into motion.

The Right Medicine

There's a play on words in our favorite prayer. The word *eleison* sounds like another Greek word, *elaion*, which means "olives" or "olive oil." In the first century, olive oil was medicinal. If the sun scorched your skin or if you had an irritated wound, you would sooth it with olive oil. The pharmaceutical practitioners of the day used it as a base to mix with other medicine in hopes that they could bring healing or at least alleviation to people's afflicted bodies. Most likely the blind men following Jesus had tried an olive oil concoction or two on their eyes.

When they said, *Kyrie eleison*, it sounded like *Kyrie elaion*. "Lord, have mercy on me," sounded like, "Lord, have medicine on me." Lord, bring healing to my life. Because sin isn't the only reason we ask for mercy.

We seek mercy after the doctor informs us about our cancer. During the chemotherapy we pray the mercy prayer hoping that God will lessen the nausea. Or when, after going through a painful divorce, you still have to work with each other for the sake of the children.

When Jesus touched the two blind men and healed them, the first face they ever saw was the face of Jesus. It reminds me of blind Fanny Crosby's reasoning that when she gets to heaven the first face she will have ever seen will be that of Jesus. For these blind beggars, that dream became a reality in this life.

Then Jesus said, "See that no one knows about this." He looks them in their brand-new eyes and says essentially, "I have a favor to ask of you: Don't let anybody know. When you leave here, don't tell anybody I did this." This isn't an uncommon request for Jesus. I think the reason is that his miracles were intended to point to the kingdom, but people so easily got distracted by miracles and missed the kingdom. And so he says, "I did this for you. I had mercy on you. Just do me a big favor. When you leave here, don't tell anyone I did this for you."

But when God has mercy, how do you keep your mouth shut? When God is merciful to you, how do you hold that in? So they walked out of there, and you can imagine what happened. The news leaked out everywhere.

"He is merciful! He is merciful! The Son of David had mercy on me." The Scripture says, "They went and spread the news about him all over that region" (Matt. 9:31). And note the word *region*; even without social media, this news spread far and wide. For when you have experienced the mercy of God, you just can't keep it to yourself. Thus Jesus' reputation of compassion grew.

What Do You Want?

These two blind men were healed up north near Capernaum. Yet word traveled all the way south to another town, Jericho. Two more blind men in Jericho heard about the arrival of the merciful Son of David, and they desired the same thing. They hoped Jesus wouldn't pass them by.

> As Jesus and his disciples were leaving Jericho, a large crowd followed him. Two blind men were sitting by the roadside, and when they heard that Jesus was going by, they shouted, "Lord, Son of David, have mercy on us!"
>
> The crowd rebuked them and told them to be quiet, but they shouted all the louder, "Lord, Son of David, have mercy on us!"
>
> Jesus stopped and called them. "What do you want me to do for you?" he asked.
>
> "Lord," they answered, "we want our sight."
>
> Jesus had compassion on them and touched their eyes. Immediately they received their sight and followed him. (Matt. 20:29–34)

This was their one shot. Notice the desperation in their plea. Jesus was coming through, and they started screaming at the top of their lungs. They didn't know where he was, but they knew he was nearby, and they started making a commotion. The crowd shushed them, but they started shouting all the more.

Why? Because there are some things you can only get from Jesus. They could get charity from others.

They could get kindness from strangers on the street, but mercy needs to come directly from God. God was walking by, so they wanted to get his attention and begged, "Lord, have mercy." *Kyrie eleison!*

These two men didn't have to chase Jesus. He took a different approach this time, and Christ came to them. The question he posed was different as well. To the first two, he had asked, "Do you believe?" To these two, he asked, "What do you want me to do for you?"

Wasn't it obvious? They're blind. They wanted to see. And yet he asked, "What do you want?" Jesus didn't assume their lack of sight was what they wanted him to address.

How would you answer that question? What do you want Jesus to do for you today? If he were going to remove something from your life, what would it be?

The blind men were to change a course of events they didn't want to take place in their lives. They might have thought, *The dominos are falling, and we don't like it. We don't want to be blind the rest of our lives. We want you to deal with our sight.*

I have a friend who oftentimes says, "You must want what your wants lead to." Jesus said essentially, "What do you want? You want to see? To want to see means you don't want to be a beggar anymore. To not be a beggar anymore means you want to go get a job. To get a job means you want to be a productive member of society and be a blessing to others." We must want what our wants lead to. We must want a certain course of action to take place in our lives. And so he said to them, "What do you want me to do?"

He didn't assume he knew the answer, and he let them say what their true desire was, because sometimes people find advantages in our disadvantages. Sometimes we find abilities in our disabilities. Sometimes there's something in our lives about which everybody would say, "Surely, you want that taken away." But the secret is, we are actually fine with it. The pain and inconvenience aren't good, but we like the perks that come along with the apparent hassle. We like the extra attention we get. We like the extra sympathy. We like the way people wait on us hand and foot, because sometimes, our disadvantages have advantages. Do we really want Jesus to step in and take them away? Or do we have a weird sort of romance with them?

Do we want what our wants lead to?

One scholar and poet who was also an alcoholic writes about his struggle with alcohol. When he didn't have a drink, he describes it as every atom in his body screaming out for this substance. He felt horrible when he didn't have a drink, as if his whole body cried and shrieked to have alcohol. One of his friends, after reading his poetry, said, "Why don't you go get treatment?" He answered, "No, that's how I feel, but that doesn't mean I want to be cured."[2]

That's the way it is with sin sometimes. Dallas Willard confronts us with our true motives when he writes, "Yet, I must do one or the other. Either I must intend to stop sinning or *not* intend to stop. There is no third possibility. I must plan to follow Jesus fully or not plan to follow him."[3]

Do I intend to quit? If not, then that means I intend to keep sinning! We don't actually say this out loud, yet the reason we don't plan on repenting is that we like what sin brings into our lives. We like what the writer of Hebrews called "the pleasures of sin" (Heb. 11:25).

So Jesus came to the blind men and said, "What do you want me to do for you?"

They replied, "We want to see." He touched them, and they could. They stood up. They followed.

Let's make the questions of Jesus personal:

1. Do you believe he is able to be merciful?
2. What do you want him to do?

As we've seen, answering those questions could lead you closer to an experience of God's compassion and grace. They are the questions that Christ asked right before doing the seemingly impossible in these men's lives. They could be the start of your own encounter with the miracle of the mercy of Christ.

O Gentle Savior

Do you believe in his mercy? What do you want him to do for you? If you could ask Jesus for mercy now, what would you ask him for?

While it is true that Jesus never turned down a request for mercy, we need to be careful not to put self-imposed restrictions on him. Yes, he genuinely wants to know what we want him to do for us, but ultimately we must trust that he knows what is best.

If we don't trust, we might ask for mercy and become disappointed when nothing changes in our lives.

That thing you're asking him to take away may be there tomorrow and the next day and even a year from now; and in those moments when you can't see what God has done, you start saying, "Did I not have enough faith? Was the problem me? Or did I ask for the wrong thing? Was I using my sin to get something so Jesus didn't respond?"

Also in those moments we're prone to turn blame inward and say, "I'm just a horrible Christian." We must guard against this. God is most merciful *and* most mysterious; we can't make him do what we want him to do. Sometimes no response is the most merciful response Jesus can give.

The two sets of blind men who sought Jesus for mercy can offer us insight into this. Notice the differences. The second pair said, "Have mercy." Jesus came to them and gave them sight. The first two said, "Have mercy," and Jesus didn't immediately come to them. They remained blind, *yet they still followed.*

Perhaps the state we are in is actually a form of mercy, though we might not be able to tell. Could it be that the blind men, in their blindness at that moment before he ultimately healed them, were already experiencing God's mercy? What brought these men to Jesus? Their blindness. Why did they ask for mercy? Their blindness. Why did they keep following? Their blindness. Why did they pursue him indoors? Their blindness. It was their blindness that kept them coming to Jesus—just as sometimes our pain and our circumstances are the very reasons we're in church, the very reasons we pray and seek him.

Are you experiencing the consequences of your own sin, and you want your Judge to step in to remove a domino and finally bring an end to the consequences? Are you suffering the consequences of someone else's sin? Does your spouse want a divorce? Did a drunk driver forever alter your life? Ask Christ for mercy and hear him ask you just what he asked the blind men: Do you believe I am able to be merciful? What do you want me to do?

One time Fanny Crosby sat in church and heard someone whispering next to her, "Don't pass me by." She then wrote these words about the mercy of God:

Pass me not, O gentle Savior,
Hear my humble cry;
While on others Thou art calling,
Do not pass me by.

Savior, Savior,
Hear my humble cry,
While on others Thou art calling,
Do not pass me by.

Let me at Thy throne of mercy
Find a sweet relief;
Kneeling there in deep contrition,
Help my unbelief.

Savior, Savior,
Hear my humble cry,
While on others Thou art calling,
Do not pass me by.

Trusting only in Thy merit,
Would I seek Thy face;
Heal my wounded, broken spirit,
Save me by Thy grace.

Savior, Savior,
Hear my humble cry,
While on others Thou art calling,
Do not pass me by.

Thou the spring of all my comfort,
More than life to me,
Whom have I on earth beside Thee,
Whom in Heav'n but Thee.

Savior, Savior,
Hear my humble cry,
While on others Thou art calling,
Do not pass me by.[4]

Remember, though it may appear that Jesus is passing you by, he has never failed to respond to the most prayed prayer. As a matter of fact, hard as it may be to see, our current state may be a result of his mercy as well.

SIX

On the Border

Jesus sought out places of tension and turmoil. He put himself in places where pain reigned unchallenged and suffering created unusual bonds. Most people avoid places like this; thankfully, Jesus embraced them—for in such space, mercy flows freely.

Now on his way to Jerusalem, Jesus traveled along the border between Samaria and Galilee. As he was going into a village, ten men who had leprosy met him. They stood at a distance and called out in a loud voice, "Jesus, Master, have pity on us!" When he saw them, he said, "Go, show yourselves to the priests." And as they went, they were cleansed.

One of them, when he saw he was healed, came

back, praising God in a loud voice. He threw himself at Jesus' feet and thanked him—and he was a
Samaritan. Jesus asked, "Were not all ten cleansed?
Where are the other nine? Has no one found to
return and give praise to God except this foreigner?"
Then he said to him, "Rise and go; your faith has
made you well." (Luke 17:11–19)

The author of this brief account, the physician
Luke, is very specific about the travel itinerary of Jesus.
He notes that Jesus was "on his way to Jerusalem."
Given that this was the last year of Christ's ministry,
and Jerusalem was the location of his crucifixion, that's
another way of saying he was on his way to die. On his
way to be betrayed and arrested. On his way to face
trumped-up charges and mock trials. On his way to
being blindfolded, spit upon, and beaten. On his way
to the cross.

Jesus, on his way to die in Jerusalem, takes a rather
odd route. Luke says, "Jesus traveled along the bor-
der between Samaria and Galilee." He walked on the
border—a place of tension and turmoil because the
Jews in Galilee did not like the Jews of Samaria. At all.
Their hatred dated back to a war between Samaria and
Assyria. The Assyrians won, and over time diluted the
Samaritans' culture and identity. The Jews in Galilee

looked down on the Jews in Samaria because of this. They called them half-breeds and dogs because they had unthinkably intermarried with the enemy. They regarded them as spiritually inferior because, in their estimation, they worshiped in the wrong place (on the sacred mountain instead of the temple in Jerusalem) and with incomplete scriptures (they only had the first five books of the Old Testament).

Despite this history and the ongoing animosity, Jesus chose to walk on the border because he loves everyone, even those caught in the tension of generations of conflict. He was on his way to die for all people, even the Samaritans. Showing no favoritism, he traveled this way because his cross would erase distinctions of superiority and inferiority and bring peace to our divisions. Along the way, he ran into an atypical group of people: ten men with the disease of leprosy.

Their skin had open sores oozing with a foul-smelling pus. Their voices were hoarse, and when they breathed it sounded like a wheeze. They were in horrible physical condition. Jesus crossed paths with these men whose hair was falling out and whose eyebrows no longer existed. Regardless of their age, they would live for about nine years in this condition. They, too, were on their way to die.

Leprosy had made them social outcasts as well. In

addition to all that was not right with their bodies, they were also in poor standing with society. They were no longer allowed in the community. They were no longer permitted to live in their own houses. Because they were considered unclean, they were forced to live in isolation. If the wind was blowing, they had to be at least fifty yards away from people. That's why they kept their distance from Jesus.

The Bond of Suffering

The group's ethnic makeup is surprising: nine Jews and one Samaritan. Their collective pain brought them together. Societal barriers don't mean as much on the border; for there, suffering unites.

In the wild, when a flood sweeps through an area, animals will head for high ground. You might see a hyena, lion, and antelope all standing side by side on high ground—predator and prey; but because of the common tragedy they are experiencing, there is peace among them for a moment. That's similar to what is happening in these verses.

Jews and a Samaritan living in community. The border is a place where new realities and new relationships can take place. The border is a place where Jesus went because he was dying for all; and the border is a place where we find groups of people crying out for mercy.

I think the border is what Christ desires his church to be. Church is meant to be a place where we find community, often because of our weaknesses. In the body of Christ, odd groups of people gather and find unity, each of us with our own addictions (drugs, alcohol, sex, pornography, food, approval, and spending money we don't have) and idiosyncrasies (our needs to control, avoid, and escalate) and love—for God and each other. Side by side we sing, young and old, rich and poor, black, brown, beige, and white, because suffering unites. Ultimately, though, it's not *our* suffering that brings us together, but the suffering of Christ—for the cross brings people together regardless of our differences.

Church should be a place where you join hands in prayer and are intrigued and surprised by how much lighter or darker, wrinkled or smooth the skin of the person next to you is. Where someone's accent when saying "Amen" is different from yours. The Scriptures say that in heaven every language and tribe and nation are gathered around the throne of God (Rev. 7:9). The church says, "on earth as it is in heaven."[1] We want it now.

Jesus shows us how to engage a world full of borders. Like Jesus, we find ourselves searching for the "border zones" as we drive hundreds of miles to Biloxi,

Mississippi, so we can rebuild the home of a man who is still homeless after Hurricane Katrina. Or as we purchase a brothel in Cambodia and transform it into an orphanage. Church is best when it mimics the ways and follows in the footsteps of Jesus. God loves all people; and, at the same time, he has a special heart for the poor and the poor in spirit, the miserable and the marginalized of society. Those on the borders of life.

While we know of folks on the borders, some of us have lost our way. Our hearts are good and we want to care when it comes to the needs of the world, but we don't know where to go. We read in the parable of the good Samaritan about a man who was left for dead on a dangerous road known as the Jericho road. We grimace as two religious leaders (the people we think should immediately come to the man's aid) see the man's need and yet do nothing. We celebrate as the Samaritan stops and enters into the injured man's life. We want to be like that man, but usually we fear we are more like the first two. It isn't that we aren't compassionate. No, it's that we no longer know where to find the Jericho road. At times, truth be told, we don't want to know where the road is. Intentionally or not, we have removed ourselves from the border zones of life.

That's why we need Jesus to show us the way.

Sometimes it's as simple as a bike ride around our neighborhood, or a five-minute walk through the apartment complex we live in. Other times all we need to do is drive to a neighborhood we usually avoid and have coffee and conversation in the local coffee shop. Or instead of going to church on a Sunday morning, go to the local skateboard park. You might discover that there are a whole lot of kids at the park (and not at home) because what they are really looking for is family, and they are finding it among fellow misfits. Ask the Spirit for the eyes of Jesus, to see the pain in this world and the places where suffering creates unusual bonds, and rediscover the Jericho road.

When we follow Jesus, not only will he lead us to the border, but he will show us what to do when we get there.

Love Up Close

We have been looking at incidents in the Bible that illustrate the mercy prayer. Every time someone comes to Jesus with a request for mercy, he pays attention. The ten lepers are no different. They "called out in a loud voice, 'Jesus, Master, have pity on us!'"

Here we see yet another nuance of the mercy of God. The word *have mercy* (*eleison*) is translated "pity."

When we say that God is merciful, we mean the Lord

is compassionate and gracious and slow to anger, abounding in love (Ps. 86:15). Now we can add an additional term to the end of that list: *pity*. If you're looking for a definition of *pity* or *compassion*, or even *mercy*, it is love in action. That's what these leprous men needed. When they said, "Have pity on us," they weren't hoping Jesus would just feel bad for them. They were hoping he would step in and actively alleviate their misery. They wanted Jesus to get involved and do something.

When God has mercy on us, he demonstrates his compassion. He actively pours his loving-kindness into our lives. To receive mercy is to receive pity and the active, engaged love of God.

Pity draws you close enough to someone's life and circumstances that you are able to feel along with them. When moved by pity, you identify with another person's pain and love them as you would want to be loved if you were living that person's life. That's also what Jesus was doing on the border. He became like the outcasts. They were considered unclean, and as Jesus walked on the border between Galilee and Samaria, guess what became true of his life?

If he had put his foot on the Samaritan side, he would have been considered an outcast as well. The religious leaders of the day considered the Samaritans unclean in the eyes of God. Jesus risked being seen as an outcast by association—a chance he was willing to take because he chose to love up close.

Jesus calls us to do the same. When the Samaritan stopped to help the man on the Jericho road, it was an act of mercy. To have compassion meant that he had to risk his life, for it was quite possible that the robbers were still nearby. I'm sure his shirt was stained with the man's blood when he lifted him onto his donkey and transported him to safety. To have compassion is to let someone else's life rub off on us. In the same way that Jesus was willing to become unclean, we, too, enter in and allow the pain of others to enter into our lives. This is the essence of being salt, as Jesus calls us.[2] Salt slows down decay, but only when it is in contact with rotting meat. Christianity is not meant to be a sanitary religion.

We follow in the footsteps of Christ, a man who hung on a cross and was mangled, marred, and scarred. The ground beneath him was bloodstained. That's to be our vision for what it means to follow Christ and to show mercy—that somehow we, too, will get messy. We serve a God who, on page one of the Scriptures, has his hands in the dirt creating us. We also are to roll up our sleeves and get involved in the muck and the mire of this world. We touch what others don't want to, and we do so with no regard for what might rub off on us.

Early Christians were not afraid of the ugliness of

this world, nor did they avoid it. This kind of thinking actually led first-century Christians to go into the garbage collection business. "Instead of evading the ugly realities of [their] time, the Christian embraced them. By doing willingly what pagans sedulously avoided . . . [they] visited the sick; [they] comforted the widow and the orphan; [they] redeemed the ignominies of starvation and sickness and squalor."[3] The early Christians dug through the local trash heaps and "collected and individually buried the bloated, diseased bodies people tossed into the garbage."[4] They did so because every life matters and death deserves honor. This required that they consider their own needs and desires as secondary.

No Thanks?

This story of Jesus on the border teaches us much about vital aspects of following Christ, such as faith, true acceptance, and gratitude.

Faith

The lepers asked for pity, and Jesus responded. He didn't say, however, "You're healed." Instead he said, "Go, show yourselves to the priests" (Luke 17:14). After all, if they were healed, the first thing they'd have to do is go see a priest for his stamp of approval. Once the priest said, "Yep, looks like you're healed!" and oversaw their cleansing ceremonies, they could enter back into society. Once declared clean they could return home, be present in their children's lives, and get jobs.

Did you notice Jesus said, "'Go' . . . And as they went, they were cleansed" (v. 14)? He said "Go," and they went even though they weren't yet healed. Because "faith is being sure of what we hope for and certain of what we do not see" (Heb. 11:1), God gave them a word, and they went, no questions asked. They believed. As they went, they were healed. That's faith.

True Acceptance

When these ten men presented themselves to the priest, they were going to be declared healed and clean. Except for the Samaritan. Nine of them would be able to enter back into mainstream society, but the tenth was a Samaritan with leprosy, and after being healed, he would still be a Samaritan. His nationality wasn't changed. Even without leprosy, he was considered an outcast. He was cleansed, yet still considered unclean. He needs something more than just external healing.

The Samaritan returned and discovered what was available to all the lepers: true acceptance by God. He came back to Jesus because what good is it to have your life cleaned up and not have Christ, the one who truly accepts you? Jesus declared, "Rise and go; your faith has made you well" (Luke 17:19). Jesus accepts us for who we are, as we are.

Gratitude

What is most striking about this story is that only one of the ten men returned to give thanks. Jesus even asked, "Were not all ten cleansed? Where are the other nine?" (Luke 17:17). Are you ready for that? Our biggest fear is not that we will be declared contaminated or an outcast. No, our fear is that we will step out of our comfort zones. Love lavishly, demonstrate care and compassion, sacrifice, and no one will even notice. Maybe not even those we are trying to help. Many of us have given up on going out of our way, because someone didn't say thank you the last time we did.

I speak from personal experience. Something in me needs to be recognized, and when no recognition comes, I think (or in some cases actually say to the person), *You could at least say thank you!* That is the compensation we expect for the love we offer others. We fear that what happened to Jesus will happen to us. We must be prepared for this. He was on his way to Jerusalem, traveling on the border, and had incredible compassion on ten men, nine of whom walked away and never thanked him.

If we're going to love like Christ, I think we should

just assume 90 percent of people we go out of our way to help will never respond in the way we hope. Ninety percent of people will not say thank you. They might even fight you. They might even yell.

Notice Jesus didn't call the other nine back and unheal them. He didn't take back his mercy. He healed all ten even though nine showed no gratitude, and then he still went on to Jerusalem. He still suffered. He still died for all of them and all of us. It was the greatest act of mercy for the world. And I think it's safe to say, in two thousand years, the majority of human beings on this planet have not said thank you. Yet he is still merciful.

Mercy in Disguise

We have much to learn about faith, acceptance, and gratitude from this passage, but let's not miss out on what else we learn about mercy: sometimes it is painful to receive.

Sheldon Vanauken (Van) and Jean Davis (Davy) loved each other deeply. Theirs was the kind of love full of passion and poetry. They even shared journals to document their relationship and declare their love. Van wrote,

> To be in love, as to see beauty, is a kind of adoring that turns the love away from self. Just seeing Davy asleep, defenseless and trusting and innocent, could

tear my heart, then in that first spring or a dozen years later. When we first fell in love in the dead of winter, we said, "If we aren't more in love in lilac-time, we shall be finished." But we *were* more in love: for love must grow or die. Every year on our anniversary we said, "If we're not more deeply in love next year, we shall have failed." But we were: a deeper inloveness, more close, more dear.[5]

Van called their tender love a "pagan" love, for it was a selfish obsession. They pledged to put nothing above their affection for each other. That included children. Because they could not share the experience (primarily motherhood) equally, they decided not to have any kids. Their married dream was to build a boat so that they could be together, always together, seeing the world. They named the boat *Grey Goose* because, in Van's words, "Not only wild nature and a water bird, but a lover: the grey goose, if its mate is killed, flies on alone forever."[6]

Their love, in addition to excluding children, also excluded God. Avowed agnostics, they couldn't understand how anybody would believe such trash. Especially Christianity. They thought the story of Jesus to be nothing more than a myth. Yet they were frequently puzzled by how people they respected believed it to be more. Sheldon put it this way: "What was so odd was that quite a lot of people, not just sheep but highly intelligent people, *did* apparently believe it."[7] For years Van and Davy thought, "Could there be more?" and yet concluded, "Oh, but there can't be!" But in order to be intellectually honest they decided to look into it.

Unexpectedly, their love was "invaded by Christ." One day Van came home to find tears streaming down his wife's face. In an attempt to describe her encounter with God, she wrote these opening lines of a poem that would remain unfinished:

All the world fell away last night,
Leaving you, only you, and fright.[8]

Together they began to read the Scriptures and the works of Leo Tolstoy, G. K. Chesterton, and C. S. Lewis. The latter, Lewis, would become more important to Van than he ever imagined when, on a whim, he wrote Lewis to ask questions about Christianity.

Van and Davy not only studied a great deal but also began to see Christians differently. Van wrote in their journal, "The best argument for Christianity is Christians: their joy, their certainty, their completeness. But the strongest argument *against* Christianity is also Christians—when they are somber and joyless, when they are self-righteous and smug in complacent consecration, when they are narrow and repressive, then Christianity dies a thousand deaths."[9] He concluded that while they could condemn some Christians, those Christians did not represent all Christians, nor did they represent the true teachings of Jesus. They could not condemn Christianity itself because of them.

Slowly and together, Van and Davy had what they called their "Encounter with light," describing that moment when they realized Christians weren't what they thought them to be and transitioned from thinking Christianity couldn't possibly be true to realizing that, far from being impossible, it is probable. In their words, "They came together into one, into focus, and the Light fell upon them."[10]

For Sheldon, "Light fell" when he realized he could not go back. Before they began their exploration of the ways of Christ, he would have said that he "neither accepted nor rejected Jesus, since I had never, in fact, encountered him. Now I had." To move on meant an "either or decision" and so he said, "Today, crossing from one side of the room to the other, I lumped together all I am, all I fear, hate, love, hope; and, well, DID it. I committed my ways to God in Christ."[11] All was good and right. "Davy and I, with our closeness of understanding and love, made an almost perfect team."[12]

And then the unthinkable happened. Davy died. Sheldon grieved and, involuntarily, learned a difficult truth about the mercy of God.

This may feel like I'm shifting the focus, but let's return to a question from above: Why did the nine lepers not thank Jesus? My guess is they were surprised by how painful God's mercy could be. When you have leprosy, you can't feel. You could take a needle and stick it in your finger. You wouldn't feel it. How did they know they were healed? How did they know Jesus had mercy on them? How did they know their leprosy was gone? Their sense of feeling returned. The leprosy was gone, but now the finger they broke yesterday throbbed with pain. Because of God's mercy, they were in more pain than they had been in years.

Thankfully, Sheldon had C. S. Lewis to help him sort through this difficult reality. They'd begun exchanging letters when Davy was exploring Christianity. Surprisingly (to them), Lewis responded. When Davy died, Lewis became an indispensable comfort to Van. He leaned on Lewis through his tears and honest questions.

Because he loved Davy so much, he didn't want to waste her death. He resolved to bear the pain and "find the whole meaning of it, taste the whole of it. I was driven by an unswerving determination to plumb the depths as well as to know the Davy I loved: to understand why she has lived and died, to learn from sorrow whatever it had to teach."[13] In the process, he found himself standing in the painful shoes of the healed lepers.

C. S. Lewis gently led Sheldon to see that perhaps Davy's death was actually God's mercy in disguise. Sheldon had to face the fact that after his wife fell in love with Jesus and began giving her life to him, he was jealous. Their vow to put no one above each other was broken, and he was angry. Though he didn't admit it until after her death, if her life had continued and her love for God grown, Van would have tried to lessen her relationship with God in order to regain his status as number one in her life. Or, worse, he would have come to hate God (or Davy). Once Lewis helped Sheldon face his jealousy of God, he helped him see that, painful though it was, God's mercy—a severe mercy—may have been at work.

Later in life Sheldon reflected that this is not a concept with "immediate appeal." After all, "Here were two young people in their thirties who loved each other . . . how can her death be seen as a *mercy*?"[14] Yet Sheldon came to agree with Lewis that Davy's death "was, precisely, a severe mercy. Our love *had* to perish, Lewis says. Perish in its earthly form, at least . . . Perish [so that] it could be redeemed."[15]

The Pain of Healing

This is not an easy or desirable aspect of God's mercy. We might come to God for pity and that pity may be painful. But sometimes that is precisely what healing feels like.

I'm reminded of Job's words after his wife told him to "Curse God and die!" His response: "Shall we accept good from God, and not trouble?" (Job 2:9–10).

What a statement. Are we willing to accept *whatever* comes our way if it comes from God? The sting of alcohol on a wound or the painful prick of the nurse's needle are good in light of their contexts, yet no less painful. When we ask God for mercy, if pain arrives, we must press in—no, we must *run* to God—for it may be his healing hand at work.

Even in that moment, let us be sure to return and give thanks to our God.

SEVEN

Strings Attached

Jesus spent a great deal of time communicating and demonstrating the mercy of God. He said, "Blessed are the merciful, for they will be shown mercy" and "Be merciful, just as your Father is merciful" (Matt. 5:7; Luke 6:36). His mission was a mission of mercy. Still, some missed the point.

As Jesus went on from there, he saw a man named Matthew sitting at the tax collector's booth. "Follow me," he told him, and Matthew got up and followed him. While Jesus was having dinner at Matthew's house, many tax collectors and "sinners" came and ate with him and his disciples. When the Pharisees saw this, they asked his

disciples, "Why does your teacher eat with tax collectors and 'sinners'?" (Matt. 9:9–11)

Matthew dropped everything at Jesus' invitation
and decided to throw a party so all his associates could
meet his new friend. The religious leaders crashed the
party and began to interrogate the disciples: "How is it
a good thing that Jesus attend this party?" "Why does
he socialize with sinners?"

Jesus, overhearing the cross-examination, decided
to give his questioners a homework assignment. "It is
not the healthy who need a doctor," Jesus said to them,
"but the sick. But go and learn what this means: 'I desire
mercy, not sacrifice'" (Matt. 9:12–13). He gave them a
Bible verse to look up. Literally. It's an exercise he hoped
would awaken their appetites and lead them to become
students of God's mercy.

They parted ways and Jesus continued his mission
of mercy. A little while later, you'll remember, two blind
men chased him and cried out, "Have mercy on us." Jesus
granted their request (Matt. 9:27–34). It wasn't long before
he met up with the Pharisees again, and the question was,
had they completed their homework assignment?

At that time Jesus went through the grainfields on
the Sabbath. His disciples were hungry and began

to pick some heads of grain and eat them. When the Pharisees saw this, they said to him, "Look! Your disciples are doing what is unlawful on the Sabbath." (Matt. 12:1–2)

Always quick to point out what they thought was wrong in someone else's life, the Pharisees picked up where they left off with Jesus. I love Christ's response. Instead of arguing he simply pointed out that they didn't do their assignment: "If you had known what these words mean, 'I desire mercy, not sacrifice,' you would not have condemned the innocent" (Matt. 12:7).

Jesus called them out. He wanted them to look at a verse in the book of Hosea and learn from it, and they had failed to follow through on his simple request. Ultimately, Jesus was asking them to become students of the mercy of God, and they missed it.

Go and Learn

When we commit to the study of mercy, we learn so much about God's heart. We discover that God has plentiful stockpiles of mercy and he delights in doling it out.

Right from the beginning pages of Scripture we see his mercy on display. Adam and Eve do wrong, but God lessens the consequences of their sin by covering their shame and nakedness. This theme recurs again and again throughout the rest of the Bible.

When we become students of mercy, we quickly discover the value of the mercy prayer. As we have seen, a cursory reading of the Scriptures reveals that this is the one prayer prayed more than any other. This has led some to seek God's mercy with every beat of their hearts.

Do you remember your assignment from chapter 3? Have you tried it yet? If not, give it a shot the next time you go to sleep. Make sure the TV and radio are off. In those quiet moments before unconsciousness, when you can feel, almost hear, the beat of your heart, begin to pray, "Lord, have mercy . . . Lord, have mercy . . . Lord, have mercy" in unison with your beating heart. Many people have discovered that if you build this prayer into the rhythm of your body, you find yourself dreaming about mercy. It just becomes part of you. My experience is that when I stir in the middle of the night, God's mercy is my first waking thought; and when I rise in the morning, his mercy is the first thing on my mind.

This practice takes persistence, but I'm sure that if you give it time you will find out what so many others have: the most prayed prayer in the Bible can be *your* most prayed prayer too.

Remember, "Lord, have mercy *on me*" is only one

way to end that prayer. We can also plead, "Lord, have mercy *on my aunt Susan*" or "*on my mother*" or "*on my daughter.*" This was modeled for us when a distraught father approached Jesus on behalf of his suffering boy. You'll remember that he looked at Jesus and said, "Lord, have mercy," but he didn't end his request with "on me." Rather, he said, "Lord, have mercy *on my son*" (Matt. 17:15, emphasis added).

Here we see the potential of this prayer. Here we realize why we want to learn to pray this prayer with every beat of our hearts. There is such great need for mercy in this world. It isn't that we personally need all that mercy; only a few of those heartbeats need be spent on ourselves. The rest are meant for our family, our friends, and the world. We build this prayer into our lives so our automatic responses to the next major earthquake or tsunami are, "Lord, have mercy." When the cry of our hearts is for mercy, we find ourselves in constant communion with God for the needs of others both near and far.

The Pharisees didn't understand this, so Jesus tried to encourage them to become students of the mercy of God. He encourages us to do the same. If we become students of God's mercy, I believe we will ultimately build the most answered prayer into our communion with God. It will forever change our relationships with God—and each other.

Love Mercy

How would your relationships be different if mercy were built into them? If you were a student of God's mercy—that is, if mercy became a way of life—how would it transform your relationship with your family? Your coworkers? Your neighbors?

I remember reading a story about twin brothers who lived years ago. Together from before birth, they were close, seemingly bonded for life. In childhood they were inseparable; and when they grew up, the towns-people said the reason they never married was because they loved each other so much.

When their father died, they took over the family business and ran it together. One day, one of the broth-ers was so busy that instead of fully ringing up one customer before he moved on to help the next person in line, he left a dollar bill sitting on top of the cash regis-ter. Later he remembered the misplaced bill, but when he went back to the cash register, the money was gone.

He asked his brother, "Did you take the dollar bill I left there?"

"No, I didn't," came the reply.

Unable to let the matter go, he asked again, "Surely you took it. There was no one else in the store." Again, the other brother denied taking the money and became angry.

It became a point of tension between them. Distrust arose; angst grew; anger and combativeness set in. Over time, the accusations and defensiveness led to a rift that ultimately got out of hand. Shockingly, they proceeded to build a partition down the center of the store, and they ran separate businesses out of their respective sides.

Decades passed, and then one day a nice car with out-of-state plates drove up. A well-dressed man walked into one side of the store and asked, "Have you been in business very long here?"

The brother answered, "Yes, thirty or forty years."

"Good," continued the stranger, "I very much need to tell you something . . . Some twenty years ago, I passed through this town. I was out of work and home-less. I jumped off a boxcar. I had no money and I had not eaten for days. I came down that alley outside and when I looked into your store window, I saw a dollar bill on the cash register. I slipped in and took it. Recently I became a Christian. I was converted and accepted Christ as my personal Savior. I know now it was wrong of me to steal that dollar bill . . . and I have come to pay you back with interest and to beg your forgiveness."

The brother, with tears in his eyes, took the man to the other side of the store so he could tell the story to his estranged brother.[1]

Now that's a bit on the dramatic side, but what

about you and me? What about our relationships? How much time have we lost in our relationships because mercy did not reign? How would things have been different if we had done Jesus' homework assignment? Not only does mercy change how we relate with God, but it also has a spillover effect in our relationships with each other. Too many fathers and sons, mothers and daughters, husbands and wives have lost weeks, months, even years for the lack of mercy.

Mercy is meant to change our relationships with not only God but also each other.

I remember reading a moving story of mercy in marriage. It was about a woman who served faithfully in her church and was a strong Christian. She also had a secret: years ago she had been unfaithful to her husband without him knowing. She shared this with her pastor, seeking his advice. If the marriage was stable and the incident was well in the past, his usual counsel in situations like this was to leave it in the past. However, knowing the life and faith of her husband, the pastor sensed that the best course of action in this case was for her to confess.

A week later the pastor, "eager to know the outcome . . . asked her about her husband's response. With joy she told him that upon telling her husband the regretful ordeal, her husband responded, 'Honey, I've known all this time.'"[2]

That kind of mercy and forgiveness is the result of truly doing one's homework! If we become students of God's mercy, we will see that mercy transforms the way we talk to God and treat our loved ones. This is why Jesus said essentially, "Go. Study. Learn what it means that God desires mercy." That is, devote time (like you are doing right now!) to understanding what it means to be compassionate, gracious, slow to anger, and abounding in love. And apply it.

In the Old Testament book of Micah, we find some helpful advice about becoming a student of God's mercy:

> With what shall I come before the LORD and bow down before the exalted God? Shall I come before him with burnt offerings, with calves a year old? Will the LORD be pleased with thousands of rams, with ten thousand rivers of oil? Shall I offer my firstborn for my transgression, the fruit of my body for the sin of my soul? (Mic. 6:6–7)

The prophet asked in summary, "What does God want from me?" The answer? "He has showed you, O man, what is good. And what does the LORD require of you? To act justly and to love mercy and to walk humbly with your God" (Mic. 6:8).

I love that last sentence. What does God want? In

addition to doing justice and walking humbly with God, we are to *love* mercy. When we walk humbly with God, mercy becomes a life companion. As the psalmist said, "Surely goodness and mercy shall follow me all the days of my life" (Ps. 23:6 NKJV).

Loving mercy makes Jesus' homework assignment a delight. When Christ called the Pharisees to become students of mercy, he wasn't asking them to study mercy the way you study for an exam in school. You study something one way when you are trying to earn a good grade, and an entirely different way when you study something because you love it.

I remember the first love letter my wife wrote me. I still have it. It is seven handwritten pages of sheer delight! I was full of anxious anticipation the first time I opened the thick, sealed envelope and unfolded the pages. I read through it as fast as I could. All I wanted to do was get a grasp of what she was saying. But that wasn't the only time I read it. No, I slowly reread it many times. Each sentence captivated my heart. I noticed variances in vocabulary: *She said "love" on this page, but "like" on another. I wonder if there are any implications behind that. What does that mean? Does she like me or love me?* Studying that letter was not a duty but a delight.

When you study something you love, it is an exercise of the head and heart. When you love someone, you can't wait to learn more about him or her. Because I love my wife, I have become a student of her ways, her smile and sleeping habits, her eyes and her laugh. I examine her ways and her whys, her dreams and her desires with the hope of meeting and exceeding them. (Don't tell her, but after all these years of gazing into her eyes, I've become a pretty good student of them. I'm no artist but I can sketch from memory the unique contours of both; each with their separate number of eyelashes. That's what love does to you!)

Love influences the way we examine and learn about something. The same is true with mercy. When God calls us to love mercy, he knows that love makes all the difference. The reason this is so important is that loving mercy is an essential part of the triad of what God requires of us: Do justice. Love mercy. Walk humbly with God.

Do It Now

We are to walk humbly with God and do justice, but notice that mercy is the link between the two. As we walk with God, we gain vision for how we can do great things with God. We begin to see the world not as it is but as it should be. We begin to ask God, "If you could change one thing in the world through me, what would it be?" God responds, and with him we begin to do justice. We roll up our sleeves and start cleaning up polluted streams. We get involved in our local schools to curb the low graduation rates. We start petitions that draw attention to the extremely high abortion rate of Down syndrome babies.

Walk with God and fight for justice, but realize the essential link between holding on to the hands of a great God and allowing him to do great things in this world through you: *love mercy*. Oftentimes we start dreaming so big about what God can do with our lives that we end up missing the great things that can be done in small ways. Mercy makes justice practical. Mercy drives us to ask, What can I do in the name of Christ today?

You've heard the old adages: "Give a man a fish, and he'll eat for a day; teach him to fish, and he'll eat for a lifetime" and "He who owns the lake feeds the village." That captures how we think when we do justice. We want to teach people to fish. If we teach someone to fish really well, not only will he eat for a day, but he can catch a few other fish and feed his family as well. If he can get a loan to buy a boat and make some nets, then he can start a business and maybe even buy the lake. If he buys the lake, then he'll feed a whole village. We want to make big systemic changes in this world. Nothing wrong with that; but mercy reminds us, as we teach a man to fish, we shouldn't forget he's hungry. So give him a fish for today, and then get on with the lesson.

Mercy makes justice practical and concrete. Mercy makes love count now. When showing mercy, ask yourself, *What does this person need right now? Devoid of my dreams of the future, how do I have compassion and grace and loving-kindness today?* Love God. Love what he might do through you to change this world, but love mercy as well.

This is how Jesus operated. He came to be the bread of life, but on the way to being the bread of life for the whole world, he fed thousands of people some physical bread one day. True, they were hungry later, but his actions were merciful in the moment. When we become students of mercy, it drives us to loving now. We don't know if we're going to have tomorrow, so we love today as if we were Christ loving people: urgently. Mother Teresa was right in saying that what this world needs is for us to do "small things with great love." That's mercy, simply doing small things with God's great love flowing through us. I'm sure Mother Teresa saw great things that needed to be done. She served in India with its oppressive caste system and stifling poverty. Sure, she would have loved to solve those problems. Yet driven by compassion she walked out of her door and loved the person right there in front of her. The person suffering at her doorstep who needed just a little water in his mouth as he faded from this life to the next.

So what does it mean to act as such a student of mercy? We must realize God has great love available and wants it to channel through us into people's lives today. It's not about the future; it's about what we can do to be merciful now. For when we go to God and say, "Have mercy on me," we're not asking somewhere in the future. We're saying, "*Now!* I need your love now." This world needs love now, not us planning on loving somebody someday. Our cities and neighborhoods need God's people to love today.

So walk with God and do justice, but love mercy now. Right now. When God gives you a chance to love, don't delay. Students of mercy know love is not meant to be put off; love is given in the moment. Look again at Jesus' words to the Pharisees: "It is not the healthy who need a doctor, but the sick. But go and learn what this means: 'I desire mercy, not sacrifice.' For I have not come to call the righteous, but sinners" (Matt. 9:12–13).

He equates sin with sickness. Mercy drove Jesus to see himself as a doctor. Doctors address problems now, not down the road.

I know a woman named Teresa whose heart breaks over Uganda, over what has happened in a country that suffered years of oppression and violence at the hands of a dictator named Idi Amin. Teresa went to this country and was captivated by the beauty of the place and the people. However, she was also distraught when she saw the ravages of sin and injustice, the poverty and the plight people are living in.

She looked at that; then when she came back to the United States she started trying to figure out, *What can I do? What great thing can I do in Uganda? I live in America.* Christians in America are some of the wealthiest Christians who ever walked the face of the planet. So what can we do for God? She began to pray. Then she remembered that little parable of the starfish. It goes like this.

There once was a boy walking on the shore of the ocean, and he came upon a beach covered in starfish, stranded and washed up by the tide. So he just picked one up and threw it back in the water to save its life. As he walked, he'd just pick up a starfish and throw it back in, one after the other. Somebody came along and said, "What are you doing?" The boy said, "I'm saving the starfish." The other said, "There are thousands of them out here. What difference can you make?" Yet the boy grabbed another starfish, threw it in, and said, "It made a difference for that one."

That's mercy. Mercy brings us to the point that even in the midst of all the pain, all the suffering, we say, "I would love God to use me in a great way to change all this, but I do know what I can do is love this one right here."

That's what mercy did in my friend Teresa's life when she asked, "What can I do in Uganda?" In Uganda countless numbers of girls will become pregnant as teenagers, some because of their own promiscuity and even more because of rape and incest. What do you do when you know right now one million teenage girls are going to be violated and have children to carry and raise in a country you can fly to in less than a day? You let mercy make your love practical. Teresa and her team started the Starfish Program. It's an educational scholarship plan that addresses the needs in the lives of a mother and child right now.[3]

In this world, we hear about pain and suffering everywhere. We want to do great things but don't know how to do them. But if we become students of mercy, we become like Jesus, seeing opportunities for mercy and responding to that one person with compassion and grace. Mercy gets our feet wet. In the midst of walking with a great God and dreaming of great things God can do through us, mercy says, "But what are you going to do today in the name of Christ? How are you going to love today?"

That's one of the reasons I'm so grateful for my wife, Barbara. I'm a dreamer. I'm always talking about what we're going to do and the great things we could accomplish in this world. Do you know there are half a million children in the foster care system in America?

I want to change that. I see a day when America has no children in the foster care system. A few years ago in Colorado there were almost nine hundred children in our foster care system who were ready for adoption. Children without parents, waiting for homes. So I began to dream, "Honey, do you see how we could solve this? There are fifteen hundred churches in the Denver metro area. If every church took one child, you'd have a waiting list of families, not a waiting list of children!" I began to plan and strategize.

Barbara, in addition to dreaming big, picked up a pen and filled out the adoption paperwork for social services. She decided we needed to love now. While I was dreaming about the capacity of all the churches in Denver, she was dreaming about the capacity of our family. Eventually we started a ministry called Project 127 with the purpose of emptying Colorado's foster care system. But along the way, we also built our family through adoption. God has blessed us with six children (one biological, five adopted—three from foster care, two from Ethiopia) because of my wife's merciful heart.[4]

As We Also Have . . .

Peter asked, "Lord, how many times shall I forgive my brother when he sins against me? Up to seven times?"

(Matt. 18:21). Peter thought he was being generous because the rabbis taught that you only needed to forgive three times. So Peter decided to double that and add one for good measure. By offering to forgive someone seven times, he thought he was going above and beyond. Then Jesus shocked everyone by saying, "I tell you, not seven times, but seventy-seven times" (v. 22).

Essentially our Savior is saying we should not put limits on our forgiveness. God has no boundaries on how many times he forgives. Neither should we. This is directly related to our understanding of mercy. God never runs out of mercy; his loving-kindness is renewed every morning. Thus it is imperative that we understand how God's mercy comes with strings attached.

When I pray the Lord's Prayer, one line always gives me pause because of four little words: "as we also have." Those words stop me in my tracks because they tie my actions to the actions of God. Jesus taught us that we should pray, "Forgive us our debts, *as we also have* forgiven our debtors" (Matt. 6:12, emphasis added). God's mercy comes to us with the condition that we also will be merciful. If we are willing to receive mercy, then we are agreeing to be dispensers of mercy; that is, we will be slow to anger and quick to offer compassion, grace, and loving-kindness. This is why Jesus continued his answer on forgiveness by telling the parable of the unmerciful servant, in which he invites us to imagine a man who owes a debt he cannot pay.

> Therefore, the kingdom of heaven is like a king who wanted to settle accounts with his servants. As he began the settlement, a man who owed him ten thousand talents was brought to him. (Matt. 18:23–24)

Ten thousand talents! That is more than he could earn in one thousand lifetimes (think billions of dollars).[5] Yet when he was informed of the natural consequences of his predicament, namely that all that he had and all that was important to him (including his wife and children) were to be sold, he simply thought he needed more time: "Be patient with me . . . and I will pay back everything" (Matt. 18:26). We all have had those moments of irrational reasoning when we actually think we can gain for ourselves what only God can give. How many of us have had a conversation with a friend about heaven only to discover that they actually think they can be good enough to get there? When we gently remind them of the debt of our wrongdoings, they think all they need is more time to make the good of their life outweigh the bad. How many of us know someone like this? How many of us are like this? Thankfully God thinks differently.

The unreasonable servant didn't know the true nature of his king. The king, in addition to being just, was also merciful—and his mercy trumped his justice! Even though the servant didn't ask for mercy, mercy was given. "The servant's master took pity on him," the story says, "canceled the debt and let him go" (Matt. 18:27).

As I said earlier, if we become students of God's mercy, I believe we will ultimately build the mercy prayer into our communion with God. If we do, it will forever change our relationships with God *and* each other. Receiving mercy is meant to transform us into dispensers of mercy. That's the point Jesus drove home with the second half of the parable.

> But when that servant went out, he found one of his fellow servants who owed him a hundred denarii. He grabbed him and began to choke him. "Pay back what you owe me!" he demanded. His fellow servant fell to his knees and begged him, "Be patient with me, and I will pay you back." But he refused. Instead, he went off and had the man thrown into prison until he could pay the debt. (Matt. 18:28–30)

This man demanded the repayment of a few dollars right after his unfathomable debt was forgiven. The unreasonable servant is now the unmerciful servant. His fellow servant asked for extra time using the man's exact same words, yet those words had no effect. Instead of granting mercy as he had received mercy, the forgiven servant demanded what was owed. He wanted justice.

His fellow servants were distressed. Mercy should alter the way we deal with those around us, and they knew it. That's why the other servants reported to the master what happened. The king was incensed and had the first servant thrown in prison.

Jesus told this story so we can have insight to our just and merciful King: "This is how my heavenly Father will treat each of you unless you forgive your brother from your heart" (Matt. 18:35). Yes, God delights to show us mercy; but when we receive God's mercy and don't then offer it to others, we are placing ourselves in a grave predicament.

I'm sure the man sat in jail and rationalized, "Why should I give up my rights just because the king gave up his?" The king had the right to collect his debt and chose not to. Does that really require that the man should forfeit his rights? For the rest of his life, whenever someone owed him should he just let him or her off the hook? In Jesus' mind the answer is a resounding *yes*! In the parable, the king asked the ultimate rhetorical question when he said, "Shouldn't you have had mercy on your fellow servant just as I had on you?" (Matt. 18:33). Translation: "Don't you know that mercy comes with strings attached?"

If we want to be recipients, we simultaneously take on the responsibility to offer mercy to others. If we are going to say, "Lord, have mercy on me," by receiving it, we are saying to the people in our lives—our families, friends, neighbors, coworkers, and children—"Because I have received mercy, you can expect that I will be merciful to you. I will be compassionate and gracious, slow to anger, abounding in love."

Such is life in the kingdom of God. As James the brother of Jesus said, "Judgment without mercy will be shown to anyone who has not been merciful. Mercy triumphs over judgment!" (James 2:13). If the Pharisees had completed their homework assignment they would have discovered this. God delights to show mercy, and he also expects us to do the same. On the one hand this is sobering for anyone who endeavors to pray the mercy prayer. We should pause and ask God to reveal anyone from whom we are withholding mercy and then act quickly to remedy the problem. We need to embrace the fact that mercy takes precedent over our rights. But while this should sober us, let's not let it stop us!

EIGHT

Let Us

J esus said to his disciples, "Let us go over to the other side" (Mark 4:35). And with that they jumped in their boats and set sail across the Sea of Galilee. The crowds Jesus had been teaching followed along in other boats. Suddenly, the winds began to blow, throwing waves into the boat. Some of the disciples bailed water while the others went looking for Jesus. Where was he? What was Jesus doing? *Sleeping!*

They woke him up saying, "Teacher, don't you care if we drown?" Jesus got up and—with mere words—brought an end to the storm.

"Why are you so afraid?" he asked. "Do you still have no faith?" (Mark 4:40). Translation: "There's no change in plans. Didn't I say, 'Let us go over to the other side'?"

The disciples stood in amazement, even somewhat terrified, but resumed their positions on the boat. And from there they continued to sail, now calmly, to the other side.

Why did Jesus want to go? What was so important that he took his disciples (and all the people in the other boats) out into a storm? The answer: On the other side was a man in need of God's mercy (Matt. 8:28; Mark 5:1; Luke 8:26).

On the other side was a man who used to be a child who ran freely with his friends but became isolated and alone. At one time he had dreams, but now his waking and sleeping hours were filled only with nightmares. We have more questions than answers. How did the forces of darkness gain a foothold in his life? What did he do? What was done to him?

All we know is that he suffered from demon possession and lived in the caves alongside the sea. Many had tried to subdue him with chains, but he only broke free with extraordinary strength. He lived isolated from people—tormented by the demons. Ken Gire eloquently summarizes the situation: "Now his body is a beachhead for Satan. And it is onto this beachhead that Jesus now lands."[1]

Not only did Jesus have the power to calm the storm, but he wanted to bring peace to this man's life as well. In Jesus we see that God's mercy is also proactive. We aren't told that the man asked for mercy and then Jesus responded. In this case, Jesus sought this man out to alleviate his suffering. The result was that this man, after his encounter with Jesus, was restored to his right mind, and when he wanted to leave with Jesus in the boat, Jesus said, "Go home to your family and tell them how much the Lord has done for you, and how he has had mercy on you" (Mark 5:19).

What I find most interesting about this story isn't that a man received mercy even though he didn't ask for it. No, what I find most shocking is *who* in the story prayed the mercy prayer.

What's Stopping Us?

Let's walk through this slowly. When Jesus arrived on the shore, the man, seeing him from a distance, ran to him. Jesus immediately commanded the unclean spirit, "Come out of this man, you evil spirit!" (Mark 5:8). And then the unthinkable happens.

We are told that the man fell on his knees before Jesus. This was not an act of worship but an act of deference—it is recognition that Jesus is the one in charge, that Jesus is the Lord.

It becomes evident that this man is under the

control of the powers of darkness when he speaks. As a matter of fact, he is possessed not by one spirit but by scores of spirits. We know this because when Jesus asks, "What is your name?" the spirits reply, "My name is Legion for we are many" (Mark 5:9). A Roman legion consisted of roughly five thousand soldiers. This man was truly suffering!

The dialogue between Jesus and Legion is astonishing. The man shouted at the top of his voice, "What do you want with me, Jesus, Son of the Most High God? Swear to God that you won't torture me!" (Mark 5:7).

The spirit used his personal name, "Jesus." Demons have known Jesus their whole lives. He created them. This encounter is not their first (they knew Christ before the manger) nor will it be their last.

The spirit recognized Jesus' position and power when it bowed and said, "Son of the Most High God." Here we have the beginnings of the mercy prayer. The blind men said, "Have mercy on us, Son of David!" (Matt. 9:27). The Canaanite woman said, "Lord, Son of David, have mercy on me!" (Matt. 15:22). The father of the demon-possessed boy with seizures prayed, "Lord, have mercy on my son" (Matt. 17:15). The second set of blind men prayed, "Lord, Son of David, have mercy on us!" (Matt. 20:30). The ten lepers stood at a distance and called out in a loud voice, "Jesus, Master, have pity on us!" (Luke 17:13).

Each time, there was recognition of the person and position of Christ. And each time Jesus stopped and responded to their request. No one who came to Jesus with this request went away unsatisfied.

So what about Legion? Will Jesus respond even to demons' request for mercy? Would a demon even ask? The man knelt: *Lord*. The demon called Christ by name: *Jesus*. The spirit recognized Jesus' position: *Son of God*. But does he ask for mercy? I think so. Here are the three accounts recorded in the Bible.

From Matthew:

"What do you want with us, Son of God?" they shouted. "Have you come here to torture us before the appointed time?" Some distance from them a large herd of pigs was feeding. The demons begged Jesus, "If you drive us out, send us into the herd of pigs." (Matt. 8:29–31)

From Mark:

He shouted at the top of his voice, "What do you want with me, Jesus, Son of the Most High God? Swear to God that you won't torture me!" . . . And he begged Jesus again and again not to send them out of the area. A large herd of pigs was feeding on the nearby hillside. The demons begged Jesus, "Send us among the pigs; allow us to go into them." (Mark 5:7, 10–12)

And from Luke:

When he saw Jesus, he cried out and fell at his feet, shouting at the top of his voice, "What do you want with me, Jesus, Son of the Most High God? I beg you, don't torture me!" . . . And they begged him repeatedly not to order them to go into the Abyss. A large herd of pigs was feeding there on the hillside. The demons begged Jesus to let them go into them. (Luke 8:28, 31–32)

It's clear that Legion fears a penalty. In all three accounts the demons refer to what Jesus could do to them as "torture." They are concerned that Jesus will inflict torment and harm on them for what they have done to this poor man. For them, torture would occur if Jesus ordered "them to go into the Abyss."[2] Suffice it to say, it is the ultimate punishment for these demons. What's clear is that Legion knows Jesus is his judge. The spirits recognize that the one before whom they bow has ultimate power over their existence. But they also know that as a judge he has a reputation for leniency—for mercy—and that's why they begin to beg.

Mark says they begged "again and again," and Luke uses the word "repeatedly" to describe their pleading with Jesus. What they want is for Jesus to lessen their sentence by sending them into a nearby herd of pigs. I don't pretend to fully understand this, but apparently unclean spirits like to have a place to call home. They prefer to have a body to inhabit, be it human or animal. Jesus put it this way: "When an evil spirit comes out of a person, it goes through arid places seeking rest and does not find it" (Matt. 12:43). They are trying to avoid "the Abyss" and "arid places." Again, I don't fully comprehend this, but what is obvious to me is that being sent into the pigs is their preferred option in this situation.

One has to ask, "Where does their hope come from? Why do they think this tactic of begging could work?" Legion even asks Jesus to take a vow: "Swear to God you won't torture me." How ironic. A demon wants Jesus to take an oath to God that he won't give them the ultimate penalty—yet. It is key to note that the spirits know that ultimately Jesus will lock them up for good. Their concern is that this will happen before the "appointed time." They have already been tried, convicted, and sentenced. But they haven't been ordered to turn themselves in and start serving their sentence. For some reason Jesus has allowed them to be free, even though they have been convicted. Perhaps that is where their hope comes from. They reason, "Jesus has let us run loose this long; perhaps he'll let us go a little longer." Even though the word for *mercy* is not used specifically, this is nothing short of a request for mercy.

Lord, Jesus, Son of God, please send us into the pigs instead of the Abyss. In other words, have mercy on us. Astonishing! The demons uttered their own version of the mercy prayer!

Jesus' response?

The demons begged Jesus, "Send us among the pigs; allow us to go into them." He gave them permission, and the evil sprits came out and went into the pigs. The herd, about two thousand in number, rushed down the steep bank into the lake and were drowned. (Mark 5:12–13)[3]

What? Permission granted! Everything inside of me wants to question Jesus' actions here. The demons wanted to determine their own punishment. Jesus, for the moment, lets them have their own way. *But Jesus, these are demons. Isn't this irresponsible?* If I were there I would have run screaming, "No! You can't do this. Legion hasn't repented. They will only harm and destroy again."

When the demons ran the pigs off the cliff destroying the property and livelihood of the owners, would I have stood there self-righteously and said, "See, I told you so"? Or would I have joined in with the crowd that "plead[ed] with Jesus to leave their region"? I don't know. What I do know is this: Jesus responded to the request for mercy *first* from these demons. Let me put it another way: as you read through the Gospels it is this demon known as Legion who asks for mercy first. Or another way: this incident of the mercy prayer comes before all the others. Before the blind men, the Canaanite mother, the desperate father, and the ten lepers, Legion comes and requests mercy.

If Jesus will say yes to an unclean spirit's request for mercy, then what is stopping us? Let us all get in line. Let us all make our requests. Let us all recognize that God is compassionate and gracious, slow to anger and abounding in love. Let us all get in our feeble boats of faith and brave the storm. "Let us go to the other side!"

Let Us Approach

When it came to the veil in the temple, very few were allowed to go to the other side. The veil was a large curtain covering the entrance into the Holy of Holies. In the Holy of Holies was the throne of God. Once a year, on the Day of Atonement, the high priest was allowed to go through the veil to the other side. Timidly he would stand in the presence of God. With the aroma of incense surrounding him, he would sprinkle the blood of an innocent animal. The sacrifice was for sins of God's people. This is the language the writer of Hebrews uses to describe the work of Christ on the cross:

> When Christ came as high priest of the good things that are already here, he went through the greater and more perfect tabernacle that is not man-made, that is to say, not a part of this creation. He did not enter by means of the blood of goats and calves; but he entered the Most Holy Place once for all by his own blood, having obtained eternal redemption. (Heb. 9:11–12)

When Jesus breathed his last breath on the cross, we are told that, "At that moment the curtain of the temple was torn in two from top to bottom" (Matt. 27:51). This means all of us can go to the other side. Though we were formerly barred, now, without hesitation, you and I can approach the mercy seat of God and stand in the presence of the most merciful judge in the universe.

The invitation has been extended to all: "Let us then approach the throne of grace with confidence, so that we may receive mercy and find grace to help us in our time of need" (Heb. 4:16).

Be bold in your pursuit of the mercy of God. Pray the mercy prayer with confidence and without acquiescence. Say it with a cheerfully courageous smile on your face: "Lord Jesus, Son of God, have mercy on me!"

This is precisely what the first murderer did. God saw that Cain was contemplating the unthinkable in his heart. He had an anger toward his brother that, if left unchecked, would lead to the first homicide in the history of humankind. As Cain grew nearer to a first-degree offense, God sounded the alarm: "Why are you angry? Why is your face downcast? If you do what is right, will you not be accepted? But if you do not do what is right, sin is crouching at your door; it desires to have you, but you must master it" (Gen. 4:6–7).

God posed three questions hoping to stir up self-reflection as Cain's tunnel vision narrowed. He tried to point out that what happened to his parents—Adam and Eve—is now happening to him. Sin was near. If he didn't back away, he too would know the aftertaste of evil. Still, Cain proceeded and murdered his brother. Did he bury Abel in an attempt to cover the shame of his crime, just as his parents had done?

God pursued, "Where is your brother Abel?" I think God was searching for a confession. But Cain wouldn't go there. Instead, Cain replied, "I don't know. Am I my brother's keeper?" (Gen. 4:9).

I've always loved that phrase, "brother's keeper." It reminds me of the story about Booker T. Washington when he was a young slave child. The slaves always received the leftovers, be it food or material for clothing. His shirts were made out of a rough, itch-inducing fiber. He always dreaded getting a new shirt. He compared the rubbing of the shirt against his skin to that of having a tooth pulled or a dozen burrs scrape against his young skin. Thankfully, Booker T. had an older brother who would take the new shirt upon himself and wear it until the roughness grew dull. Booker T.'s brother, John, was his keeper.[4]

Cain shirked even this basic responsibility to his brother in order to not have to admit that he was responsible for the first death of a human being. Given Cain's refusal to admit liability, God takes on the role of prosecutor and judge and presents the evidence, announces the verdict, and declares the sentence:

> Listen! Your brother's blood cries out to me from the ground. Now you are under a curse and driven from the ground, which opened its mouth to receive

your brother's blood from your hand. When you work the ground, it will no longer yield its crops for you. You will be a restless wanderer on the earth. (Gen. 4:10–12)

Cain commits premeditated murder and then refuses to admit any knowledge. God, however, does not give him the ultimate sentence of death. Why not an eye for an eye and a tooth for a tooth (Lev. 24:20)? Instead, God mercifully reduces Cain's deserved death sentence to life in isolation without parole. As Pope John Paul II said, "God, who preferred the correction rather than the death of a sinner, did not desire that a homicide be punished by the exaction of another act of homicide."[5]

For Cain, however, even this reduced sentence is too much, and he becomes the first person in the Bible to ask God for mercy. "Cain said to the LORD, 'My punishment is more than I can bear. Today you are driving me from the land, and I will be hidden from your presence; I will be a restless wanderer on the earth, and whoever finds me will kill me'" (Gen. 4:13–14).

Now that's bold! If I were Cain's lawyer I would have said, "Take the plea bargain! You just avoided the death penalty; accept your punishment." But Cain believed others would try to find him and exact vengeance.

He believed there would be a bounty on his head, and wherever he went people would try to bring him to full justice. So Cain boldly shared this with God and discovered what we now know: God is compassionate and gracious, slow to anger and abounding in love.

God said, "'Not so; if anyone kills Cain, he will suffer vengeance seven times over.' Then the LORD put a mark on Cain so that no one who found him would kill him" (Gen. 4:15). God promised to protect Cain's life even though Cain took the life of his brother. Again, Pope John Paul II:

> And yet God, who is always merciful even when he punishes, "*put a mark on Cain*, lest any who came upon him should kill him." (Gen. 4:15) He thus gave him a distinctive sign, not to condemn him to the hatred of others, but to protect and defend him from those wishing to kill him, even out of a desire to avenge Abel's death. *Not even a murderer loses his personal dignity*, and God himself pledges to guarantee this. And it is precisely here that the *paradoxical mystery of the merciful justice of God* is shown forth."[6]

So true: "the paradoxical mystery of the merciful justice of God." Cain was the first to test and prove that

God is more than willing to grant mercy to those who ask. Cain paved the way for David (the man who prayed for mercy the most), the blind beggars, the Canaanite mom, and the distraught father of the demon-possessed boy. The cast-out Cain laid the groundwork for the ten outcast lepers to present their request. It strikes me that Cain was bold *prior* to Jesus dying on the cross, rising from the dead, and presenting his blood as our great High Priest. How much more bold can we be this side of the cross and the torn veil?

Listen to the words of Hebrews again: "Let us then approach the throne of grace with confidence, so that we may receive mercy and find grace to help us in our time of need" (Heb. 4:16). Let us pray loudly with the psalmist those words found in the longest chapter in the Bible, "Turn to me and have mercy on me, as you always do to those who love your name" (Ps. 119:132).

Let Us Practice

In my book *Finding the Groove: Composing a Jazz-Shaped Faith*, I wrote about the role of practice in the Christian life.[7] Imagine we are going to a jazz club together. On the way I tell you that the person playing the trumpet has practiced that one instrument for thirty years. What would you expect? Wouldn't your hopes be high? We would anticipate hearing someone whose skills were highly developed. Perfection wouldn't be the standard, but surely it would be reasonable to look forward to an enjoyable performance. So what if I told you I have practiced following Jesus for thirty years? What should you expect of me?

It's going to take practice and commitment to build the mercy prayer into your life. Its full effect requires the devotion to weave it into the fabric of your waking and sleeping life. Paul instructs Timothy, "Train yourself to be godly. For physical training is of some value, but godliness has value for all things, holding promise for both the present life and the life to come" (1 Tim. 4:7–8). Spiritual health, like physical health, takes dedication. John Ortberg points out that there is a big difference between trying to be like Jesus and training to be like Jesus. He writes, "There is an immense difference between training to do something and trying to do something."[8] This also holds true when it comes to the mercy prayer.

One of my favorite books is the Russian mystical classic *The Way of a Pilgrim*. Written in the nineteenth century, it tells the story of a Christian wanderer who is trying to figure out how we can "pray without ceasing" (1 Thess. 5:17 NKJV). He visits a number of churches with renowned preachers and finds that for their many words, they offer no real insight. He visits a local spiritual director whose answer is full of platitudes but lacks clarity. Eventually, he is introduced to the mercy prayer in the Bible. He's told,

> Find a quiet place to sit alone and in silence; bow your head and shut your eyes. Breathe softly, look with your mind into your heart; recollect your mind—that is, all its thoughts—and bring them down from your mind into your heart. As you breathe, repeat: "Lord Jesus Christ, have mercy on me," either quietly with your lips, or only in your mind. Make an effort to banish all thoughts; be calm and patient, and repeat this exercise frequently.[9]

"As you breath." "Repeat this exercise frequently." Practice!

The pilgrim in the story then commits himself to actively learning the mercy prayer. He devotes much time and study to the mercy of God. His goal is to build the prayer into his heart. This takes a lot of commitment and focus. At times he sets out to pray the mercy prayer literally thousands and tens of thousands of times a day.

The Way of a Pilgrim is important for a couple of reasons. First, it is helpful to see that others have gone before us when it comes to living out what we see in the

Scriptures. We aren't the first to try and make the mercy prayer the most prayed prayer in our lives. Second, we see that the prayer is hard work and that we need to commit to training—practice. Practice takes time, but who has time to pray the most answered prayer thousands of times per day? Perhaps that's the wrong question.

The biblical vision of prayer has a different starting point. It's not, "How much did I pray today?" but rather, "Did I ever stop praying today?" When we think in terms of, "How much time will this take?" we miss the point of unceasing prayer. We must steer away from thinking in terms of bare minimums and pursue what is truly possible: unending, unbroken communion with Jesus. As I wrote in *Finding the Groove*, the question is, "Do you have time, or does time have you?"[10]

I'm convinced we have time. We spend an average of two hours per day in our cars. Additionally, we can be found watching television four hours each day. And then there's the time we spend online. But the question is, What do we do with the time? What does it look like to get in our spiritual "reps"?

There is another reason I have found the tale of this ancient pilgrim helpful. Up until now I've talked about praying the most prayed prayer as we sleep by building it into the rhythm of our heartbeats. For the longest time, I found I could pray through the night but then struggled with the prayer during the day. The pilgrim had a secret training aid: a prayer rope.

As he would go through his day, he would carry with him a prayer rope. A prayer rope is made of wool, for "We are His people and the sheep of His pasture" (Ps. 100:3 NKJV). Often red beads are attached to the string, representing Christ's wounds and his blood shed for us. Then there are knots. The larger prayer ropes come in the form of necklaces, usually with one hundred to five hundred knots. Also, there are smaller bracelets with thirty-three knots (one for each year of Jesus' life). While praying, "Lord, have mercy," someone ties each knot in such a way that it contains seven crosses. Intricate in design, the use of a prayer rope is simple: pray the mercy prayer with each knot.

My prayer ropes are indispensable tools for me. I use both the longer necklaces and the shorter bracelets. I don't use them every day. I've found there are seasons of my life when mercy flows easily from my heart and times when it is a struggle. When it's a struggle, I grab my prayer rope for a few weeks until the practice becomes natural again. Sometimes we need something tactile to help make our spiritual lives tangible.

Occasionally, my thumb becomes red and sore from cycling the knots through my hand. At times, my prayer rope has even worn an indentation in my thumbnail.

During those times I remember what Paul said right after "train yourself to be godly." He continued the thought by saying, "For physical training is of some value, but godliness has value for all things, holding promise for both the present life and the life to come" (1 Tim. 4:8). Runners and weightlifters expect to be sore from their training. A guitar player's calloused fingertips are an accepted by-product of hours of practicing. So what's a little soreness in my thumb as I seek to learn the most answered prayer by heart?

My prayer ropes help me in my praying for others. I have a list of people in my life whom I desire God to flood with his mercy, and so I'll pray for each of them using this method, even standing in line at the grocery store or bank. Stoplights provide the perfect moment to get a set of reps in. In the sixty to ninety seconds that I sit there, I turn off the radio and grab my prayer bracelet. I've found that over the course of a day I can seek God's mercy for each person in my family.

The prayer rope also has a cross with a tassel attached. The cross reminds us that we are only able to approach the throne of grace because of the work of Christ, and that Jesus never failed to answer a single plea for mercy. The tassel is for wiping tears from your eyes.

One time I sat at the bedside of a wonderful man named Nate who was dying of cancer. As he slept, I knelt next to him and prayed for God's mercy during the last days of his life. Tears flowed and I was grateful for the tassel.

Ultimately, the wanderer in *The Way of a Pilgrim* experienced a renewed love for Jesus.

> Finally, after a short time, I felt that the prayer began to move of its own accord from my lips into my heart. That is to say, it seemed as if my heart, while beating naturally, somehow began to repeat with itself the words of the prayer in rhythm with its natural beating . . . I stopped reciting the words of the prayer with my lips and began to listen attentively to the words of my heart . . . Then I began to experience a delicate soreness in my heart, and my thoughts were filled with such a love for Jesus Christ that it seemed to me that if I were to see Him, I would have thrown myself down, embrace His feet, and never let them go, kissing them tenderly and tearfully. And I would thank Him for His love and mercy in granting such consolation through His name to His unworthy and sinful creature![11]

When we devote ourselves to building the most answered prayer into our lives, we will renew our relationships with God and revamp our prayers on behalf of others. Learning to pray the mercy prayer will also keep us "in view of God's mercy," where true transformation takes place.

Let Us Be Transformed

Let us, in view of God's mercy, be transformed. Here's how I think it works.

We all have a story to tell, but why do we tell our stories the way we do? Have you ever experienced an event with someone, but then, as you both recounted it to your friends, your versions sounded vastly different? They contained the same facts, but they weren't the same narrative. This happens with individual events, and it also happens with the stories of our lives.

When each of us tells our life story, we usually pick one of four different plots: comedy, romance, tragedy, or irony.[12] The question when listening to someone's story is not just, "What are they saying?" but, "Why are they choosing to say it the way they are? Why do we pick one plot over another?"

For those who choose romance, the search for love and the adventure of fighting and being fought for is a beautiful plot. But, as Shakespeare has shown us, romance can easily become a tragedy. Pursuit without arrival gives way to weariness. Romantic ideals without realistic expectations can leave one disappointed and dejected. The discovery that what you want hasn't lived up to the superlative you imagined can feel tragic. The realization that in this world beauty fades and strength atrophies can lead to profound disappointment.

As far as comedy and irony go, the search for joy and comfort and the desire to have it all—life, liberty, and happiness—is the story many of us are living. There is nothing wrong with pursuing joy and pleasure. King David said it well: "You have made known to me the path of life; you will fill me with joy in your presence, with eternal pleasures at your right hand" (Ps. 16:11). Comedy is not about joy but about jokes, and when one's life is viewed as a joke, ironically, that is no laughing matter. What happens when you discover that pain can't be avoided, even if you are walking with God, and cynicism sets in?

Some psychologists believe healing and transformation happens when we understand why we choose to tell our stories the way we do. Furthermore, healing happens when we are willing to rewrite our stories with different plots. But what is the different plot? This is where the mercy prayer shines. When God responds to our request for mercy, he makes room for our stories to go in new, better directions. The facts of our lives might not change, but our views of them need to change—or rather, they need to be seen in view of God's mercy.

If you think about it, the story of Jesus could be told as a tragic romance, for God is a lover who pursues at all costs, even the death of his innocent Son. Or a comedy with an ironic twist, for the thought of God trying to communicate with us feeble creatures is humorously satirical. But, in the Bible, the story of Jesus is given a different plot. It's a plot known as *gospel*. God's mercy can take any set of facts and turn them into good news—gospel! For his mercy is "better than life" (Ps. 63:3). When we pray the mercy prayer, we are asking God to take the facts of our lives—sin, suffering, mistakes, regret, pain, frustration—and weave them into a miraculous tale of life from death.

Every person in the Bible who prayed the most answered prayer came to Jesus with a set of facts (adultery and murder, disability and blindness, disease and despair) but left with a story to tell that could only be explained by saying, "God had mercy on me!"

Simply Profound

Leo Tolstoy told the tale of three hermits who lived together on an isolated island. Their devotion to God was simple, as they lived simply. Together they prayed a straightforward unadorned prayer: "We are three; you are three; have mercy on us. Amen."

The local bishop heard about the three hermits and decided they needed in-depth training and guidance. He traveled by boat to their island in order to help them in their relationship with God. Upon arrival, though impressed with their simple prayer, he gave them proper instruction on the intricacies of talking to God. When finished he blessed them and set sail for the mainland.

Suddenly, off in the distance, he saw a bright light gliding across the surface of the water. As it got closer he could see that it was the three hermits running to him on top of the water. They boarded the ship and said, "We are so sorry but we have forgotten some of your teaching. Would you please instruct us again?"

The bishop replied, "Forget everything I have taught you and continue to pray in your old way: 'We are three; you are three; have mercy on us. Amen.'"[13]

The mercy prayer. Simple. Profound. As you weave it into the fabric of your life, may you experience the good news in the eternal mercy made available to all of us by our Father in heaven.

Notes

Chapter 1: The Most Prayed Prayer

1. Oren Yaniv, "Brooklyn Chief Prosecutor Livid with Soft Sentence Issued by Supreme Court Justice Gustin Reichbach," *New York Daily News*, February 2, 2011, http://articles.nydailynews.com/2011-02-02/news/27738722_1_chief-prosecutor-undercover-cop-illegal-guns.

2. James Montgomery Boice, *Psalms* (Grand Rapids: Baker, 1998), 3:1042.

3. Ibid., 970.

4. "Pass Me Not, O Gentle Savior," words by Fanny Crosby, 1868; music by W. Howard Doane, 1870, public domain.

5. Sherwin B. Nuland, *How We Die: Reflectons on Life's Final Chapter* (New York: Vintage Books, 1995), 134.

6. 1 John 4:8.

7. 2 Peter 3:9.

8. Brennan Manning, *The Ragamuffin Gospel* (Sisters, OR: Multnomah, 1990).

9. Jonah 1:2; 3:4.

10. Gary A. Haugen, *Good News About Injustice* (Downers Grove, IL: IVP, 1999), 73.
11. Martin Luther King Jr., *I Have a Dream: Writings and Speeches That Changed the World*, ed., James M. Washington (New York: HarperOne, 1992), 85.

Chapter 2: Echoes from Eternity

1. In the Old Testament alone, the word for *mercy* occurs almost 250 times.
2. "Blessed Assurance," words by Fanny Crosby, music by Phoebe Knapp, 1873.
3. See also 1 Chron. 16:34; 16:41 and 2 Chron. 5:13; 7:3; 7:6.
4. Arthur W. Pink, *The Attributes of God* (Grand Rapids: Baker Book House, n.d.), 83–84.
5. Brennan Manning, *Abba's Child: The Cry of the Heart for Intimate Belonging* (Colorado Springs: NavPress, 2002), 12.
6. Steve and Sally Breedlove and Ralph and Jennifer Ennis, *The Shame Exchange: Trading Shame for God's Mercy and Freedom* (Colorado Springs: NavPress, 2009), 145.
7. John Edgar Wideman, *My Soul Has Grown Deep: Classics of Early African-American Literature* (Philadelphia: Running Press Book Publishers, 2001), 376.
8. Ibid.
9. Nell Irvin Painter, *Sojourner Truth: A Life, A Symbol* (New York: Norton, 1996), 160.

Chapter 3: The Prayer of the Heart

1. A. W. Tozer, *The Knowledge of the Holy* (New York: HarperCollins Publishers, 1961), 91.
2. Ibid.
3. Some attribute this to Martin Luther and others to the archbishop Richard Trench.

Chapter 4: When You're in Need

1. For example, see Psalm 91:4.
2. Peggy Skattebo, "Riding Out the Storm," *Discipleship Journal*, July/August (2002): 45.
3. 1 Sam. 17:26–37.
4. Sharon Flake, "From Panic to Poise," *Discipleship Journal*, July/August (2002): 47.
5. See 2 Samuel 15:16; 16:22; 20:3 and I Kings 11:1–3.
6. Matt. 27:37.

Chapter 5: Nothing Less than a Miracle

1. William Barclay, *The Gospel of Matthew* (Philadelphia: Westminster Press, 1975), 1:350.
2. Ibid., 1:350.
3. Dallas Willard, *The Spirit of the Disciplines: Understanding How God Changes Lives* (San Francisco: Harper Collins, 1991), 13.
4. "Do Not Pass Me By," words by Fanny Crosby, music by W. Howard Doane, 1868, public domain.

Chapter 6: On the Border

1. Matt. 6:10.
2. Matt. 5:13.
3. Ray Bakke, *A Theology as Big as the City* (Downers Grove, IL: IVP, 1997), 192–93.
4. Ibid.
5. Sheldon Vanauken, *A Severe Mercy* (San Franscisco: Harper, 1977), 43.
6. Ibid., 51.
7. Ibid., 59.
8. Ibid., 67.
9. Ibid., 85.

10. Ibid., 84.
11. Ibid., 96.
12. Ibid., 131.
13. Ibid., 187.
14. Ibid., 211.
15. Ibid., 216.

Chapter 7: Strings Attached

1. John Claypool, *The Preaching Event*, http://www.sermons plus.co.uk/Illustrations.htm.
2. Anthony J. Carter, *Hesed: A Word Better than Life* (Baltimore, MD: Publish America, 2005), 42.
3. For more information, see the Starfish Program website at http://how101.org/starfish-program/.
4. Project 127 exists to help God's people adopt and foster in faith. To date, hundreds of children have found a forever family because of this ministry. Project 127, along with many other wonderful organizations, is working diligently to empty Colorado's foster-care system. The day is coming when there will be no children waiting for families, only families waiting for children! Find out more at project127.com.
5. The total budget of Judea/Samaria was six hundred talents. For Galilee it was three hundred talents. See also Frank E. Gaebelein, *The Expositor's Bible Commentary Volume 8* (Grand Rapids: Zondervan, 1984), 406.

Chapter 8: Let Us

1. Ken Gire, *Moments with the Savior: A Devotional Life of Christ* (Grand Rapids: Zondervan, 1998), 158.
2. Read Revelation 20 for more insight.
3. Some have argued that this is the equivalent of Jesus sending them to the Abyss, but logically that doesn't make sense

to me. How does drowning pigs equal drowning spirits? No doubt Jesus is giving the demon-possessed man visible proof that they are gone, but it also seems clear that Jesus is granting the request of the demons for a lesser punishment.

4. Anthony J. Carter, *Hesed: A Word Better than Life* (Baltimore, MD: Publish America, 2005), 30.

5. John Paul II, *The Gospel of Life (Evangelium Vitae): On the Value and Inviolability of Human Life* (Washington DC: USCCB Publishing, 1995), 19.

6. Ibid., 18.

7. Robert Gelinas, *Finding the Groove: Composing a Jazz-Shaped Faith* (Grand Rapids: Zondervan, 2009), 104–5.

8. John Ortberg, *The Life You've Always Wanted: Spiritual Disciplines for Ordinary People* (Grand Rapids: Zondervan, 1997), 46–47.

9. Andrew Harvey, ed., *The Way of a Pilgrim: The Jesus Prayer Journey* (Woodstock, VT: Skylight Paths Publishing, 2001), 17.

10. Gelinas, *Finding the Groove*, 154.

11. Harvey, *The Way of a Pilgrim*, 35–36.

12. For a scholarly look at this concept see Dan P. McAdams, *The Stories We Live By: Personal Myths and the Making of the Self* (New York: The Guilford Press, 1997).

13. Richard Foster, *Prayer: Finding the Heart's True Home* (San Francisco: HarperCollins, 1992), 80.

About the Author

R obert Gelinas is lead pastor (and resident jazz theologian) of Colorado Community Church, a multicultural, interdenominational mission in the Mile High City. He holds a BA in biblical studies and an MA in missiology from Denver Seminary. He and his wife, Barbara, live in Denver with their six children.

For more information about Robert and how you can help make the mercy prayer the most prayed prayer in your community, please visit

www.robertgelinas.net